Nicholson's

WATE
GUIDE
1 SOUTH

The waterways covered by this book are

Bridgwater & Taunton Taunton to Bridgwater
Grand Union Canal London to Birmingham
Kennet & Avon Canal Reading to Bath
Lee & Stort Navigations London to Hertford and Bishops Stortford
Monmouthshire & Brecon Canal Pontypool to Brecon
Oxford Canal Oxford to Hawkesbury Junction
Gloucester & Sharpness Canal and River Severn Sharpness to Worcester
River Thames Inglesham to Brentford
River Wey Godalming to the Thames

Other books in this series are

2 Midlands **3** North

ROBERT NICHOLSON PUBLICATIONS
GEOGRAPHIA

A Nicholson Guide

First published 1978
Reprinted 1980
Second revised edition 1981

Based on the original research and observations of Andrew Darwin and Paul Atterbury

Robert Nicholson Publications Limited
24 Highbury Crescent
London N5 1RX

Printed in England by E. T. Heron, Silver End
Witham, Essex.

ISBN 0 905522 46 X

Front cover: Working boats at Hanwell on the Grand Union. Derek Pratt.

Introduction

The waterways of England and Wales have emerged from a long period of decline into an exciting period of restoration. All over the network, disused canal arms and basins are being dredged, new marinas are being built and whole lengths of canal once left to decay, are now pleasant cruiseways. In urban areas, the 'muddy ditch' at the back of the factory is being turned into a 'linear park' for the whole community to enjoy. Credit for this new lease of life must go in turn to the many societies whose members work during their spare time campaigning, clearing and rebuilding, to those enlightened local councils who are recognising the amenity value of the waterways, and of course to the British Waterways Board.

Built originally as efficient trade routes, the network today provides a unique retreat from a noisy and impersonal world, where boaters, walkers, fishermen, those interested in natural history or industrial archaeology can peacefully enjoy the beauty and quiet isolation of these once busy waterways. There is interest for everyone in the canals: the engineering feats like aqueducts, tunnels and flights of locks; the brightly decorated narrowboats; the wealth of birds, animals and plants on the canal banks; the mellow architecture of canalside buildings like pubs, stables, lock cottages and warehouses.

This series of three guides covers not only BWB waterways, but also some navigable rivers such as the Thames and the Avon, and the privately owned Bridgewater Canal. These form essential links in popular circular cruising routes.

The maps show all necessary navigational information—bridges, locks, tunnels, junctions—and the text describes the route and services available. Boatyards are listed and indicated on the maps and there is a selection of pubs and restaurants. We hope these books will guide you successfully on your journeys as well as provide you with an insight into a very valuable part of our national heritage.

Contents

Symbols

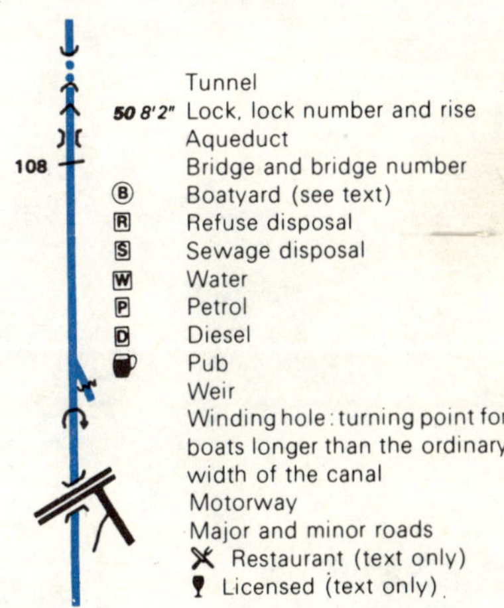

The Country Code

Guard against fire risks
Fasten all gates
Keep dogs under proper control
Keep to paths across farm land
Avoid damaging fences, hedges and walls
Leave no litter
Safeguard water supplies
Protect wildlife, wild plants and trees
Go carefully on country roads
Respect the life of the countryside

The maps are ½ inch to 1 mile scale

The distance given under the name of the section is the approximate mileage on that particular page

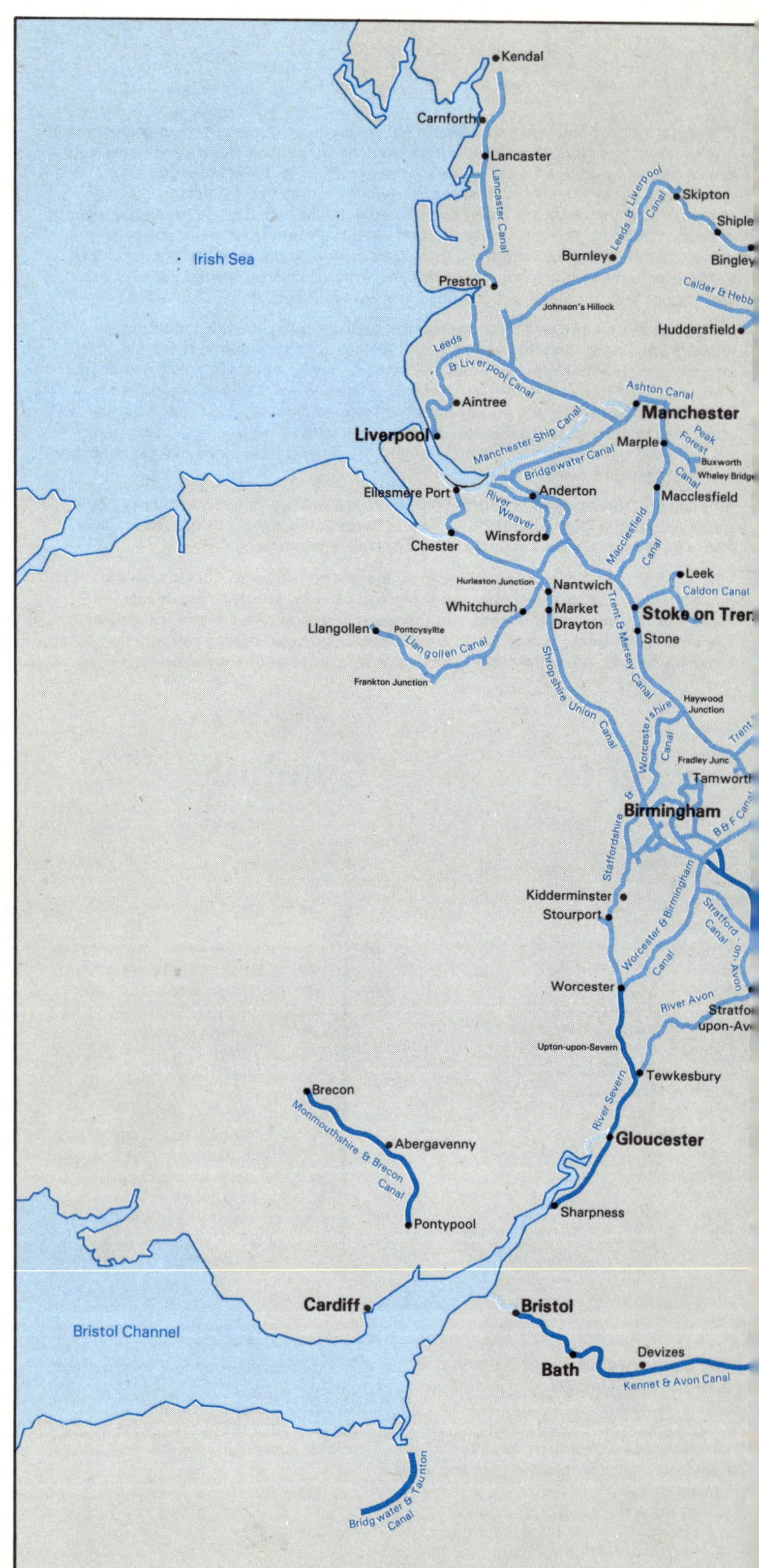
Kendal
Carnforth
Lancaster
Lancaster Canal
Irish Sea
Skipton
Leeds & Liverpool Canal
Burnley
Bingley
Preston
Calder & Hebb
Johnson's Hillock
Huddersfield
Leeds & Liverpool Canal
Aintree
Ashton Canal
Manchester
Liverpool
Manchester Ship Canal
Marple
Peak Forest Canal
Buxworth
Whaley Bridge
Bridgewater Canal
Ellesmere Port
Anderton
Macclesfield
River Weaver
Winsford
Chester
Macclesfield Canal
Leek
Hurleston Junction
Nantwich
Caldon Canal
Whitchurch
Market Drayton
Llangollen
Pontcysyllte
Llangollen Canal
Stone
Trent & Mersey Canal
Frankton Junction
Shropshire Union Canal
Haywood Junction
Worcestershire Canal
Fradley Junc
Birmingham
Staffordshire &
B & F Canal
Kidderminster
Stourport
Worcester & Birmingham Canal
Stratford-on-Avon Canal
Worcester
River Avon
Upton-upon-Severn
Tewkesbury
River Severn
Brecon
Monmouthshire & Brecon Canal
Abergavenny
Gloucester
Sharpness
Pontypool
Cardiff
Bristol
Bristol Channel
Bath
Devizes
Kennet & Avon Canal
Bridgwater & Taunton Canal

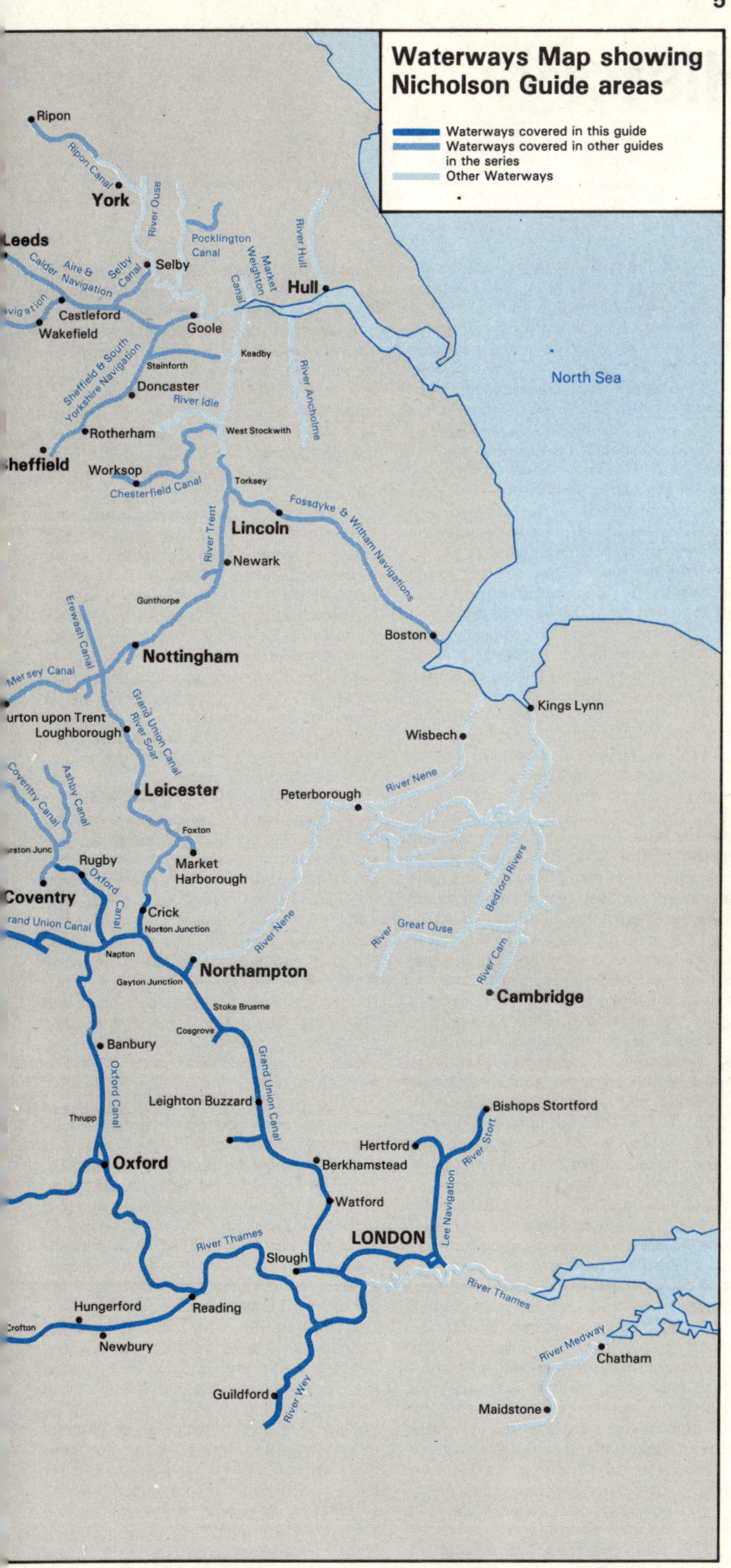

Waterways Map showing Nicholson Guide areas
Waterways covered in this guide
Waterways covered in other guides in the series
Other Waterways
North Sea
Ripon
Ripon Canal
York
River Ouse
Pocklington Canal
Market Weighton Canal
River Hull
Hull
Leeds
Selby
Selby Canal
Aire & Calder Navigation
Castleford
Wakefield
Goole
Keadby
River Ancholme
Stainforth
Sheffield & South Yorkshire Navigation
Doncaster
River Idle
West Stockwith
Rotherham
Sheffield
Worksop
Chesterfield Canal
Torksey
Fossdyke & Witham Navigations
Lincoln
River Trent
Newark
Gunthorpe
Erewash Canal
Boston
Nottingham
Mersey Canal
Burton upon Trent
Loughborough
Grand Union Canal
River Soar
Kings Lynn
Wisbech
Coventry Canal
Ashby Canal
Leicester
Peterborough
River Nene
Foxton
Market Harborough
Rugby
Oxford Canal
Coventry
Crick
Norton Junction
Bedford Rivers
River Great Ouse
River Cam
Napton
Northampton
Gayton Junction
Cambridge
Stoke Bruerne
Cosgrove
Banbury
Leighton Buzzard
Thrupp
Bishops Stortford
Hertford
River Stort
Oxford
Berkhamstead
Watford
Lee Navigation
LONDON
River Thames
Slough
Reading
Hungerford
Crofton
Newbury
River Medway
Chatham
Guildford
River Wey
Maidstone

History

River navigations, that is rivers widened and deepened to take large boats, had existed in England since the middle ages; some can even be traced back to Roman times. In 1600 there were 700 miles of navigable river in England, and by 1760, the dawn of the canal age, this number had been increased to 1300. This extensive network had prompted many developments later used by the canal engineers, for example the lock system. But there were severe limitations; generally the routes were determined by the rivers and the features of the landscape and so were rarely direct. Also there were no east-west, or north-south connections.

Thus the demand for a direct inland waterway system increased steadily through the first half of the 18thC with the expansion of internal trade. Road improvements could not cope with this expansion, and so engineers and merchants turned to canals, used extensively on the continent.

One of the earliest pure canals, cut independently of existing rivers, was opened in 1745, at Newry in Northern Ireland, although some authorities consider the Fossdyke, cut by the Romans to link the rivers Trent and Witham, to be the first. However, the Newry is more important because it established the cardinal rule of all canals, the maintenance of an adequate water supply, a feature too often ignored by later engineers. The Newry canal established the principle of a long summit level, fed by a reservoir to keep the locks at either end well supplied. Ten years later, in England, the Duke of Bridgewater decided to build a canal to provide an adequate transport outlet for his coal mines at Worsley. He employed the self-taught James Brindley as his engineer, and John Gilbert as surveyor, and launched the canal age in England. The Bridgewater canal was opened in 1761. Its route, all on one level, was independent of all rivers; its scale of operations reflected the new power of engineering, and the foresight of its creators. Although there were no locks, the engineering problems were huge; an aqueduct was built at Barton over the river Irwell, preceded by an embankment 900 yards long; 15 miles of canal were built underground, so that boats could approach the coal face for loading—eventually there were 42 miles underground, including an inclined plane—the puddled clay method was used by Brindley to make the canal bed watertight. Perhaps most important of all, the canal was a success financially. Bridgewater invested the equivalent of £3 million of his own money in the project, and still made a profit.

Having shown that canals were both practical and financially sound, the Bridgewater aroused great interest throughout Britain. Plans were drawn up for a trunk canal, to link the four major rivers of England: the Thames, Severn, Mersey and Trent. This plan was eventually brought to fruition, but many years later than its sponsors imagined. Brindley was employed as engineer for the scheme, his reputation ensuring that he would always have more work than he could ever handle. The Trent and Mersey, and the Staffordshire and Worcestershire canals received the Royal Assent in 1766, and the canal age began in earnest.

Canals, like the railways later, were built entirely by hand. Gangs of itinerant workmen were gathered together, drawn by the comparatively high pay. Once formed, these armies of 'navigators'—hence 'navvies'—moved through the countryside as the canal was built, in many cases living off the land. All engineering problems had to be solved by manpower alone, aided by the horse and the occasional steam pump. Embankments, tunnels, aqueducts, all were built by these labouring armies kept under control only by the power of the section engineers and contractors.

The Staffordshire and Worcestershire canal opened in 1770. In its design Brindley determined the size of the standard Midlands canal, which of course had direct influence on the rest of the English system as it was built. He chose a narrow canal, with locks 72ft 7in by 7ft 6in, partly for reasons of economy, and partly because he realised that the problems of an adequate water supply were far greater than most canal sponsors realised. This standard, which was also adopted for the Trent and Mersey, prompted the development of a special vessel, the narrow boat with its 30-ton payload. Ironically this decision by Brindley in 1766 ensured the failure of the canals as a commercial venture 200 years later, for by the middle of this century a 30-ton payload could no longer be worked economically.

The Trent and Mersey was opened in 1777. 93 miles long, the canal included 5 tunnels, the one at Harecastle taking 11 years to build. In 1790 Oxford was finally reached and the junction with the Thames brought the four great rivers together. From the very start English canal companies were characterised by their intense rivalries; water supplies were jealously guarded, and constant wars were waged over toll prices. Many canals receiving the Royal Assent were never built, while others staggered towards conclusion, hampered by doubtful engineering, inaccurate estimates, and loans that they could never hope to pay off. Yet for a period canal mania gripped British speculators, as railway mania was to grip them 50 years later. The peak of British canal development came between 1791 and 1794, a period that gave rise to the opening

'Navvies' (navigators) at work, removing the stop lock at Braunston in the early 1930's.

of the major routes, the rise of the great canal engineers, Telford, Rennie and Jessop, and the greatest prosperity of those companies already operating. At this time the canal system had an effective monopoly over inland transport; the old trunk roads could not compete, coastal traffic was uncertain and hazardous, and the railways were still a future dream. This period also saw the greatest feats of engineering.

The turn of the century saw the opening of the last major cross country routes: the Pennines were crossed by the Leeds and Liverpool canal between 1770 and 1816 while the Kennet and Avon, opened in 1810, linked London and Bristol via the Thames. These two canals were built as broad navigations: already the realisation was dawning on canal operators that the limits imposed by the Brindley standard were too restricting, a suspicion that was to be brutally confirmed by the coming of the railways. The Kennet and Avon, along with its rival the Thames and Severn, also marks the introduction of fine architecture to canals. Up till now canal architecture had been functional, often impressive, but clearly conceived by engineers. As a result the Kennet and Avon has an architectural unity lacking in earlier canals – incidentally another reason to justify its preservation. The appearance of architectural quality was matched by another significant change; canals became straighter, their engineers choosing as direct a route as possible, arguing that greater construction costs would be outweighed by smoother, quicker operation, whereas the early canals had followed the landscape. The Oxford is the prime example of a contour canal, meandering across the midlands as though there were all the time in the world. It looks beautiful, its close marriage with the landscape makes it ideal as a pleasure waterway, but it was commercial folly.

The shortcomings of the early canals were exploited all too easily by the new railways. At first there was sharp competition by canals. Tolls were lowered, money was poured into route improvements; 14 miles of the Oxford's windings were cut out between 1829 and 1834; schemes were prepared to widen the narrow canals; the Harecastle tunnel was doubled in 1827, the new tunnel taking 3 years to build (as opposed to the 11 years of the old). But the race was lost from the start. The 19thC marks the rise of the railways and the decline of the canals. With the exception of the Manchester Ship Canal, the last major canal was the Birmingham and Liverpool Junction, opened in 1835. The system survived until this century, but the 1914–18 war brought the first closures, and through

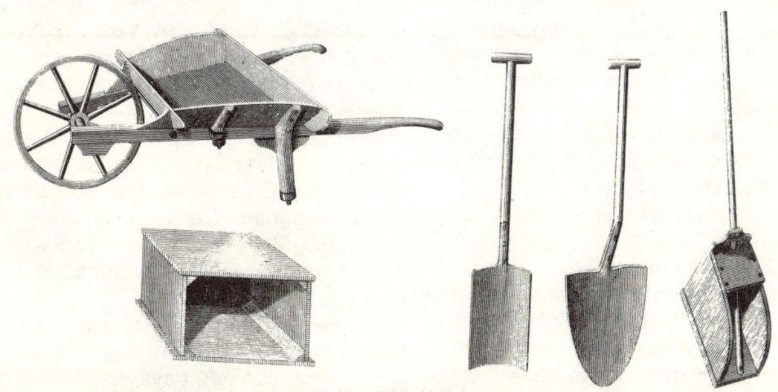

The rudimentary tools of the early 'navvies'. *Hugh McKnight.*

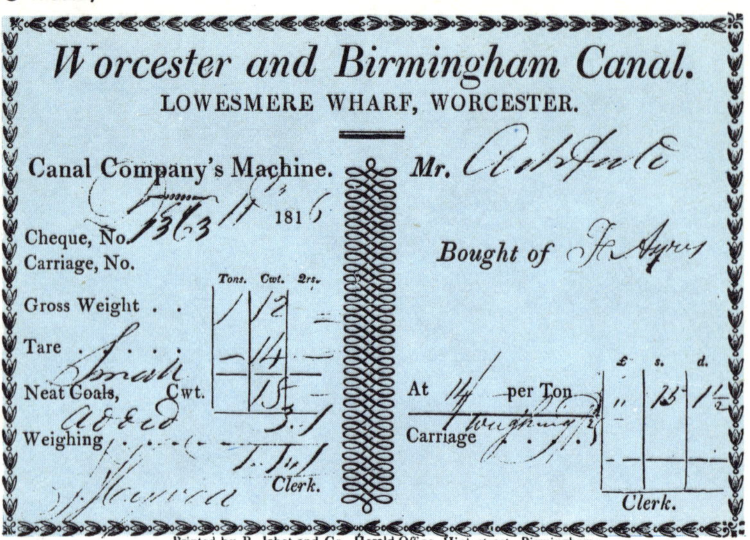

Worcester and Birmingham Canal.

LOWESMERE WHARF, WORCESTER.

Canal Company's Machine.

181

Cheque, No.

Carriage, No.

	Tons.	Cwt.	2rs.
Gross Weight . .			
Tare . . .			
Neat Coals, Cwt.			
Weighing			

Clerk.

Mr.

Bought of

	£	s.	d.
At per Ton			
Carriage			

Clerk.

Printed by R. Jabet and Co. Herald Office, High-street, Birmingham.

Worcester and Birmingham Canal Company toll ticket, dated 1816. *Hugh McKnight.*

the 1930's the canal map adopted the shape it has today. Effective commercial carrying on narrow canals ceased in the early 1960's although a few companies managed to survive until recently. However, with the end of commercial operation, a new role was seen for the waterways, as a pleasure amenity, a 'linear national park 2000 miles long'.

Water supply has always been the cardinal element in both the running and the survival of any canal system. Locks need a constant supply of water—every boat passing through a wide lock on the Grand Union uses 96,000 gallons of water. Generally two methods of supply were used: direct feed by rivers and streams, and feed by reservoirs sited along the summit level. The first suffered greatly from silting, and meant that the canal was dependent on the level of water in the river; the regular floods from the river Soar that overtake the Grand Union's Leicester line show the dangers of this. The second was more reliable, but many engineers were short-sighted in their provision of an adequate summit level. The otherwise well planned Kennet and Avon always suffered from water shortage. Where shortages occurred, steam pumping engines were used to pump water taken down locks back up to the summit level. The Kennet and Avon was dependent upon pumped supplies, while the Birmingham Canal Navigations were fed by 6 reservoirs and 17 pumping engines. Some companies adopted side ponds alongside locks to save water, but this put the onus on the boatman and so had limited success. Likewise the stop locks still to be seen at junctions are a good example of 18thC company rivalry; an established canal would ensure that any proposed canal wishing to join it would have to lock *down* into the older canal, which thus gained a lock of water each time a boat passed through.

Where long flights or staircase locks existed there was always great wastage of water, and so throughout canal history alternative mechanical means of raising boats have been tried out. The inclined plane or the vertical lift were the favoured form. Both worked on the counterbalance principle, the weight of the descending boat helping to raise the ascending. The first inclined plane was built at Ketley in 1788, and they were a feature of the west country Bude and Chard canals. The most famous plane was built at Foxton, and operated from 1900-1910. Mechanical failure and excessive running costs ended the application of the inclined plane in England, although modern examples work very efficiently on the continent, notably in Belgium. The vertical lift was more unusual, although there were 8 on the Grand Western canal. The most famous, built at Anderton in 1875, is still in operation, and stands as a monument to the ingenuity shown in the attempts to overcome the problems of water shortage.

Engineering features are the greatest legacy of the canal age, and of these, tunnels are the most impressive. The longest tunnel is at Standedge, on the now derelict Huddersfield narrow canal. The tunnel runs for 5456 yards through the Pennines, at times 600ft below the surface. It is also on the highest summit level, 656ft above sea level. The longest navigable tunnel is now Dudley Tunnel, 3154 yards, which was re-opened in 1973 after being closed for many years. Others of interest include the twin Harecastle tunnels on the Trent and Mersey, the first 2897 yards and now disused, the second 2926 yards, Sapperton which carried the Thames and Severn canal through the Cotswolds, and Netherton on the Birmingham Canal Navigation. This, built 1855-58, was the last in England, and was lit throughout by gas lights, and later by electricity.

The Netherton tunnel was built wide enough to allow for a towing path on both sides. Most tunnels have no towing path at all, and so boats had to be 'legged', or

Islington tunnel during construction. *Hugh McKnight.*

walked through.

The slowness and relative danger of legging in tunnels led to various attempts at mechanical propulsion. An endless rope pulled by a stationary steam engine at the tunnel mouth was tried out at Blisworth and Braunston between 1869 and 1871. Steam tugs were employed, an early application of mechanical power to canal boats, but their performance was greatly limited by lack of ventilation, not to mention the danger of suffocating the crew.

An electric tug was used at Harecastle from 1914 to 1954. The diesel engine made tunnel tug services much more practical, but diesel powered narrow boats soon put the tugs out of business; by the 1930's most tunnels had to be navigated by whatever means the boatman chose to use. Legging continued at Crick, Husbands Bosworth and Saddington until 1939.

Until the coming of the diesel boats, the horse reigned supreme as a source of canal power. The first canals had used gangs of men to bow-haul the boats, a left over from the river navigations where 50-80 men, or 12 horses, would pull a 200-ton barge. By 1800 the horse had taken over, and was used throughout the heyday of the canal system. In fact horse towage survived as long as large scale commercial operation. Generally one horse or one mule was used per boat, a system unmatched for cheapness and simplicity. The towing path was carried from one side of the canal to the other by turnover bridges, a common feature that reveals the total dominance of the horse. Attempts to introduce self-propelled canal boats date from 1793, although most early experiments concerned tugs towing dumb barges. Development was limited by the damage caused by wash, a problem that still applies today, and the first fleets of self propelled steam narrow boats were not in service until the last quarter of the 19thC. Fellows, Morton and Clayton, and the Leeds and Liverpool Carrying Co. ran large fleets of steam boats between 1880 and 1931, by which time most had been converted to diesel operation. With the coming of mechanical power the butty boat principle was developed; a powered narrow boat would tow a dumb 'butty' boat, thereby doubling the load without doubling the running costs. This system became standard until the virtual ending by the late 1960's of carrying on the narrow canals. Before the coming of railways, passenger services were run on the canals; packet boats, specially built narrow boats with passenger accommodation, ran express services, commanding the best horses and the unquestioned right of way over all other traffic. Although the railways killed this traffic, the last scheduled passenger service survived on the Gloucester and Berkeley canal until 1935.

The traditional narrow boat with its colourful decoration and meticulous interior has become a symbol of English canals. However this was in fact a late development. The shape of the narrow boat was determined by Brindley's original narrow canal specification, but until the late 19thC boats were unpainted, and carried all male crews. Wages were sufficient for the crews to maintain their families at home. The increase in railway competition brought a reduction in wages, and so bit by bit the crews were forced to take their families with them, becoming a kind of water gipsy. The confines of a narrow boat cabin presented the same problems as a gipsy caravan, and so the families found a similar answer. Their eternally wandering home achieved individuality by extravagant and colourful decoration, and the traditional narrow boat painting was born. The extensive symbolic vocabulary available to the painters produced a sign language that only these families could understand, and the canal world became far more enclosed, although outwardly it was more decorative. As the canals have turned from commerce to pleasure, so the traditions of the families have died out, and the families themselves have faded away. But their language survives, although its meaning has mostly vanished with them. This survival gives the canals their characteristic decorative qualities which make them so attractive to the pleasure boatman and to the casual visitor.

Cruising information

Licences

Pleasure craft using BWB canals must be licensed and those using BWB rivers must be registered under the British Waterways Act 1971. Charges are based on the length of the boat and a canal craft licence covers all the navigable waterways under the Board's control. Permits for permanent mooring on the canals are also issued by the Board. Apply in each case to:

Craft Licensing Office,
Willow Grange,
Church Road,
Watford WD1 3QA.
(Watford 26422)

The Licensing office will also supply a list of all BWB rivers and canals. Other river navigation authorities relevant to this book are mentioned where appropriate.

Getting Afloat

There is no better way of finding out the joys of canals than by getting afloat. The best thing is to hire a boat for a week or a fortnight from one of the boatyards on the canals. (Each boatyard has an entry in the text, and most of them offer hire cruisers; brochures may be easily obtained from such boatyards.)

General Cruising

Most canals are saucer shaped in section and so are deepest in the middle. However very few have more than 3-4ft of water and many have much less. Try to keep to the middle of the channel except on bends, where the deepest water is on the *outside* of the bend. When you meet another boat, the rule of the road is to keep to the right; slow down, and aim to miss the approaching boat by a couple of yards; do not steer right over to the bank unless the channel is particularly narrow or badly overgrown, or you will most likely run aground. The deeper the draught of the boat, the more important it is to keep in the middle of the deep water, and so this must be considered when passing other boats. If you meet a loaded working boat, keep right out of the way. Working boats should always be given precedence, for their time is money. If you meet a boat being towed from the bank, pass it on the outside rather than intercept the towing line. When overtaking, keep the other boat on your starboard, or right, side.

Speed

There is a general speed limit of 4mph on most British Waterways Board canals. This is not just an arbitrary limit; there is no need to go any faster, and in many cases it is impossible to cruise even at this speed. Canals were not built for motor boats, and so the banks are easily damaged by excessive wash and turbulence. Erosion of the banks makes the canal more shallow, which in turn makes running aground a more frequent occurrence. So keep to the limits and try not to aggravate the situation. It is easy to see when a boat is creating excessive turbulence by looking at the wash. If in doubt, slow down.

Slow down also when passing moored craft, engineering works and anglers.

Slow down when there is a lot of floating rubbish on the water; old planks and plastic bags may mean underwater obstacles that can damage a boat or its propeller if hit hard.

Slow down when approaching blind corners, narrow bridges and junctions.

Running aground

The effective end of commercial traffic on the narrow canals has meant a general reduction in standards of dredging. Canals are now shallower than ever, and contain more rubbish than ever. Running aground is a common event, but is rarely serious, as the canal bed is usually soft. If you run aground, try first of all to pull the boat off by reversing the engine. If this fails, use the boat hook as a lever against the bank or some solid object, in combination with a tow rope being pulled from the bank. Do not keep revving the engine in reverse if it is obviously having no effect; this will merely damage both your propeller and the canal bed by drawing water away from the boat. Another way is to get your crew to rock the boat from side to side while using the boat hook or tow rope. If all else fails, lighten your load; make all the crew leave the boat except the helmsman, and then it will often float off quite easily.

Remember that if you run aground once, it is likely to happen again as it indicates a particularly shallow stretch—or you are out of the channel.

In a town it is common to run aground on sunken rubbish, for example old oil drums, bicycle frames, bedsteads etc; this is most likely to occur near bridges and housing estates. Use the same methods, but be very careful as these hard objects can easily damage your boat or propellor.

Remember that winding holes are often silted up: do not go further in than you have to.

Mooring

All boats carry metal stakes and a mallet. These are used for mooring when there are no rings or bollards in sight, which is

How a lock works

Plan: lock filling

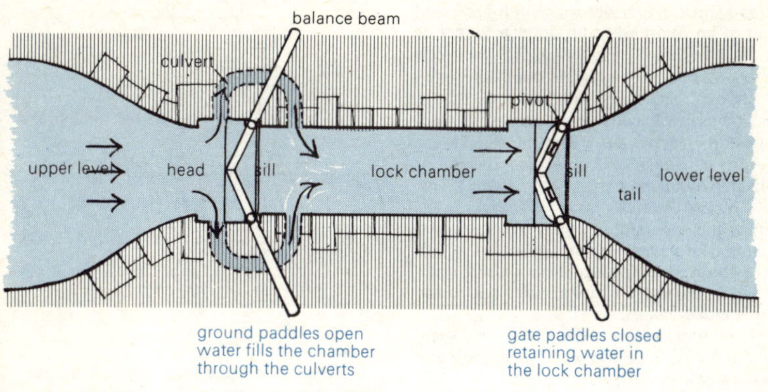

Elevation: lock emptying

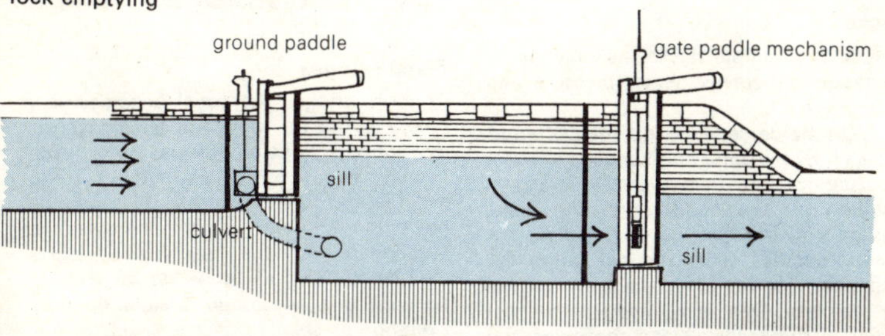

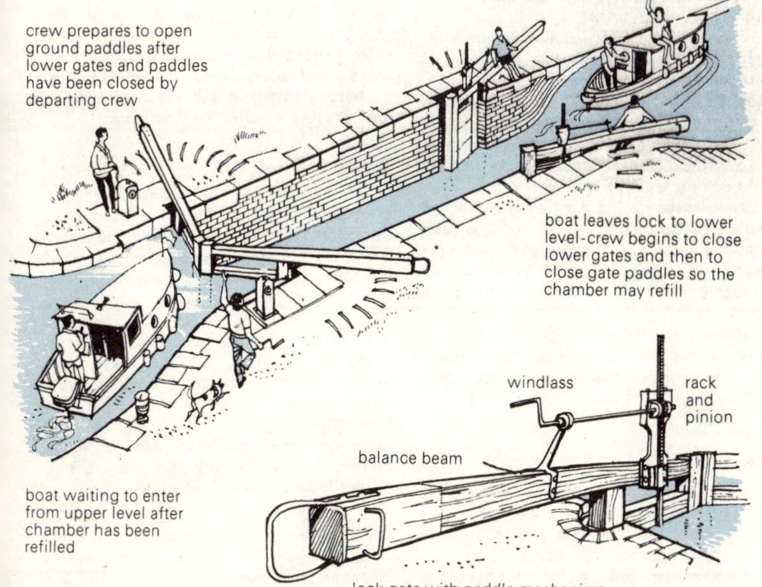

lock gate with paddle mechanism

usually the case. Generally speaking you may moor anywhere to BWB property but there are certain basic rules. Avoid mooring anywhere that could cause an obstruction to other boats; do not moor on a bend or a narrow stretch, do not moor abreast boats already moored. Never moor in a lock, and do not be tempted to tie up in a tunnel or under a bridge if it is raining. Pick a stretch where there is a reasonable depth of water at the bank, otherwise the boat may bump and scrape the canal bed – an unpleasant sensation if you are trying to sleep. For reasons of peace and quiet and privacy it is best to avoid main roads and railway lines.

Never stretch your mooring lines across the towpath; you may trip someone up and face a claim for damages.

There is no need to show a riding light at night, except on major rivers and busy commercial canals.

So long as you are sensible and keep to the rules, mooring can be a pleasant gesture of individuality.

Locks

A lock is a simple device, relying for its operation on gravity, water pressure and manpower.

On the preceding page, the plan (top) shows how the gates point uphill, the water pressure forcing them together. Water is flooding into the lock through the underground culverts that are operated by the ground paddles: when the lock is full, the 'top' gates (on the left in the drawing) can be opened. One may imagine a boat entering, the crew closing the gates and paddles after it.

In the elevation, the bottom paddles have been raised – opened – so the lock empties. A boat would of course float down with the water. When the lock is 'empty', the bottom gates can be opened and the descending boat can leave the lock.

Remember that:

1. For reasons of safety and water conservation, all gates and paddles must always be left closed when you leave a lock.

2. When going *up* a lock, a boat should be tied up to prevent it being thrown about by the rush of incoming water; but when going *down* a lock, a boat should never be tied up, or it will be left high and dry.

3. Windlasses should *not* be left slotted on the paddle spindle. If the ratchet slips (and they are often worn) the spindle will spin round and the windlass will fly off, probably into the lock or into someone's face.

4. Be very careful when operating locks in wet weather: the lockside is often slippery and the wooden planks across the gates can be downright treacherous.

Knots

You do not need to know much about knots as there is one that is generally useful, the clove hitch. This is simple, strong, and can be slipped on and off easily. Make two loops in a rope, and pass the right hand one over the left; then drop the whole thing over a bollard, post or stake and pull it tight. See diagram below.

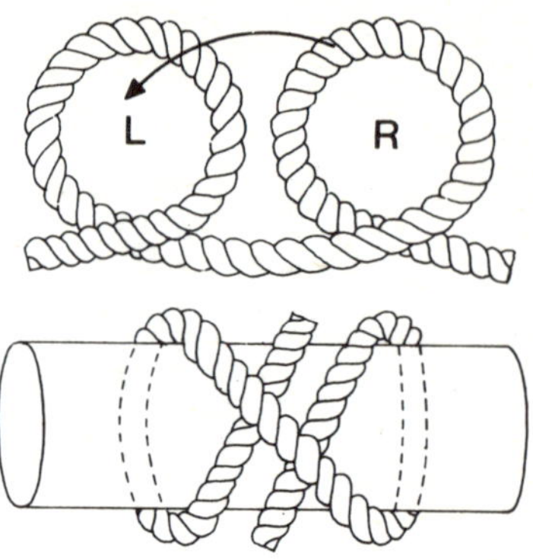

When leaving a mooring coil all the ropes up again. They will then be out of the way, but ready if needed in a hurry. Many a sailor has fallen overboard after tripping on an uncoiled rope.

Fixed bridges

At most bridges the canal becomes very narrow, a means of saving building costs developed by the engineers. As a result careful navigation is called for if you are to avoid hitting either the bridge sides with the hull or the arch with the cabin top. As when entering a lock, the best way to tackle 'bridgeholes' is to slow down well in advance and aim to go straight through, keeping a steady course. Adjustments should be kept to a minimum for it is easy to start the boat zig-zagging, which will inevitably end in a collision. One technique is to gauge the width of the approaching bridgehole relative to the width of the boat, and then watch one side only, aiming to miss that side by a small margin – say 6in; the smaller you can make the margin, the less chance you have of hitting the other side of the bridge. If you do hit the bridge sides when going slowly it is not likely to do much damage; it will merely strengthen your resolve to do better next time.

Swing bridges

Swing bridges are an attractive feature of some canals; they cannot be ignored as they often rest only 2 or 3ft above the water. Generally they are moved by being swivelled horizontally, or raised vertically. Operation is usually manual, although some have gearing to ease the movement. There are one or two mechanized swing bridges; these are very rare, and they have clear instructions at control points. Before operating any swing bridge make sure that any road traffic approaching is aware of your intention to open the bridge. Use protective barriers if there are any and remember to close the bridge again after you.

Swivel bridges, which are moved horizontally, are usually simple to operate. They do however demand considerable strength, and many are difficult for one person.

Lift bridges, which are moved vertically, are raised by pulling down a balance beam. The heaviest member of the crew should swing on the chain that hangs from the beam. Once the bridge is up the beam should be sat on or otherwise held as in some cases it fails to counterbalance the bridge. Serious damage could be caused to the boat and to the helmsman if the bridge were allowed to fall while the boat was passing through. A draw bridge is another, more traditional type of lift bridge; the method of operation is the same.

Tunnels

Many people consider a canal incomplete without one or two tunnels, and certainly they are an exciting feature of any trip. Nearly all are easy to navigate, although there are a few basic rules:

Make sure your boat has a good headlight in working order.

If you can see another boat in the tunnel coming towards you, it is best to wait until it is out before entering yourself. It is in fact possible for craft of 7ft beam to pass in many tunnels, but it can be unnerving to meet another boat. If you do, keep to the right as usual.

In most tunnels the roof drips constantly, especially under ventilation shafts. Put on a raincoat and some form of hat before going in.

A notice on the tunnel portal will give its length, in yards, and will say whether unpowered craft are permitted to use it.

Care of the engine

Canal boats are powered by one of three types of engine: diesel, petrol and petrol/oil or two-stroke. However basic rules apply to all three. Every day before starting off, you should:

Check the oil level in the engine.
Check the fuel level in the tank.

If your engine is water-cooled, check that the filter near the intake is clean and weedfree. Otherwise the engine will overheat which could cause serious damage.

Check the level of distilled water in the battery, and ensure that it is charging correctly.

Lubricate any parts of the engine, gearbox or steering that need daily attention.

Check that the propeller is free of weeds, wire, plastic bags and any other rubbish. Although this is an unpleasant task, it is a constant necessity and will remain so as long as canals continue to be used as public rubbish dumps. The propeller and the water filter should be checked whenever there is any suspicion of obstruction or overheating—which may mean several times a day.

When navigating in shallow water, keep in mind the exposed position of the propeller. If you hit any underwater obstruction put the engine into neutral immediately. When running over any large floating object put the engine into neutral and wait for the object to appear astern before re-engaging the drive.

Great respect should be shown to the engine. Remember that this simple maintenance could make the difference between trouble-free cruising and tiresome breakdowns.

Fuel

Petrol engines and petrol/oil outboards are catered for by some boatyards and all roadside fuel stations. Fuel stations on roads near the canal are shown in the guide, and these should be considered when planning your day's cruise. Running out is inconvenient; remember you may have to walk several miles carrying a heavy can.

Diesel powered boats pose more of a problem in obtaining fuel, although their range is generally greater than that of petrol powered craft. Most boatyards sell marine diesel, which is tax-free and therefore very much cheaper (the heavy tax on fuels is aimed only at road vehicles). The tax-free diesel, which contains a tell-tale pink dye to prevent it being used in road vehicles, can only be sold by boatyards, which are still few and far between on the canals. BWB yards may let you have enough to reach the next boatyard. Some, but by no means all roadside fuel stations sell diesel, but at the higher price. A further complication is that diesel engines must not be allowed to run out of fuel, as their fuel system will need professional attention before they can run again. So route planning is very much more important for owners of diesel powered craft. The simple rule about fuel is—think ahead. It is advisable to carry a spare can.

Water

Fresh water taps occur irregularly along the canals, usually at boatyards, BWB depots, or by lock cottages. These are marked on the maps in the guide. Ensure that there is a long water hose on the boat (BWB taps have a ½-inch slip on hose connection).

Lavatories

Some canal boats are fitted with chemical lavatories which have to be emptied from time to time. Never empty them over the side or just tip them into the bushes. Either empty them at the sewage disposal points marked on the maps, or dig deep holes with the spade provided. Boats with pump-out toilets must use the pump-out stations – usually boatyards and indicated in the text. Some BWB depots and boat yards have lavatories for boat crews.

Litter

Some canals are in a poor state today because they have long been misused as unofficial dumps for rubbish, especially in towns. Out of sight is only out of mind until some object is tangled round your propeller. So keep all rubbish until you can dispose of it at a refuse disposal point. (See the maps).

Byelaws

Although no one needs a 'driving licence' to navigate a boat on the waterways, boat users should remember that they incur certain responsibilities and duties, e.g. a knowledge of correct sound signals. Prospective navigators are advised to obtain a copy of the byelaws relevant to the waterways on which they are to travel.

Fishing information

This section has been written by Bill Howes, well known angling correspondent and author of many books on the subject.

Many anglers started their fishing careers on the canals, mainly because our system of waterways has always offered excellent opportunities for the thousands of angling enthusiasts throughout Great Britain.

Most of these cross-country waterways have natural reed-fringed and grassy banks, and in addition to the delightful surroundings the fishing is generally good. In most areas there has been a steady improvement in the canal fishing in recent years and in many places new stocks of fish have been introduced. Good stocks of quality bream and roach have gone into several canals in the past couple of years, and this has improved the sport considerably.

The popular quarry are roach, perch and bream, but the canals also hold dace, tench, chub and carp in places, in addition to pike and other species in particular areas.

Canals afford good hunting grounds for those seeking specimen fish, that is fish above average size, and these are liable to be encountered on almost any water, yet some areas are more noted for big fish than others. The canals also make good venues for competition fishing, and in most places nowadays matches are held regularly at week-ends throughout the season.

The Statutory Close Season for coarse fish is March 15 to June 15 inclusive, but in some areas, notably the Yorkshire River Authority, the Close Season is from February 28 to May 31. The Close Season for pike in some areas is March 15 to September 30.

Permits and fishing rights

Most parts of the waterways system are available to anglers. The big angling associations e.g. the London AA, Birmingham AA, Reading & District AA, Coventry & District AA, Nottingham AA plus many smaller clubs, rent fishing rights over extensive areas on the system. In most cases day tickets are available.

On arrival at the water-side it is always advisable to make enquiries as to who holds the fishing rights, and to obtain a permit if one is required *before* starting to fish.

Remember, also, that a River Authority rod licence is usually required in addition to a fishing permit. It is essential to obtain this licence from the relevant River Authority *before* starting to fish. Some fishing permits and licences are issued by bailiffs along the bank, but local enquiry will help to determine this.

A canalside pub or a local fishing tackle shop are good places to enquire if permission or day tickets are required for the local stretch of water. Canal lock-keepers are usually knowledgeable about the fishing rights in the immediate locality, and often a lock-keeper may be found who issues day tickets on behalf of an angling association, or owner.

A lock-keeper is always worth talking to, for apart from knowing who holds the fishing rights, he often knows some of the better fishing areas, as well as local methods and baits which may be considered most successful.

The fishing rights on most canals are owned by the British Waterways Board and many miles of good fishing are leased to clubs and angling associations. They also issue day tickets on certain lengths, so it is worth enquiring at the local British Waterways office when planning a trip. Special arrangements are made for fishing from boats. Consult BWB at Nantwich (65122).

'Private fishing' notices should *not* be ignored. If the owner's name and address is on the board then application can be made for permission for a future occasion.

Once permission has been obtained it would be advisable to find out if there are any restrictions imposed, since some clubs and associations ban certain baits, or have restrictions on live-baiting for pike; and on some fisheries pike fishing is not allowed before a specified date.

Other restrictions may concern size-limits of fish, and this certainly applies to the London AA canal fisheries. Some River Authority by-laws prohibit the retention of under-sized fish in keep nets. A local club holding the fishing rights may have imposed their own size-limits in order to protect certain species. Such restrictions are generally printed on permits and licences.

Tackle

In the slow moving, sluggish waters the float tackle needs to be light and lines fine in order to catch fish.

When fishing for roach and dace lines of 1½lb to 2lb breaking strain are the maximum strength normally needed in order to get the fish to take a bait—particularly when the water is clear, or on the popular reaches which are 'hard-fished'.

Fine tackle also means small hooks, and hook sizes 16 and 18—or even as small as 22 at times. Such light gear is also effective when fishing for the smaller species, such as gudgeon and bleak. This tackle will require a well-balanced float to show the slightest indication of a bite.

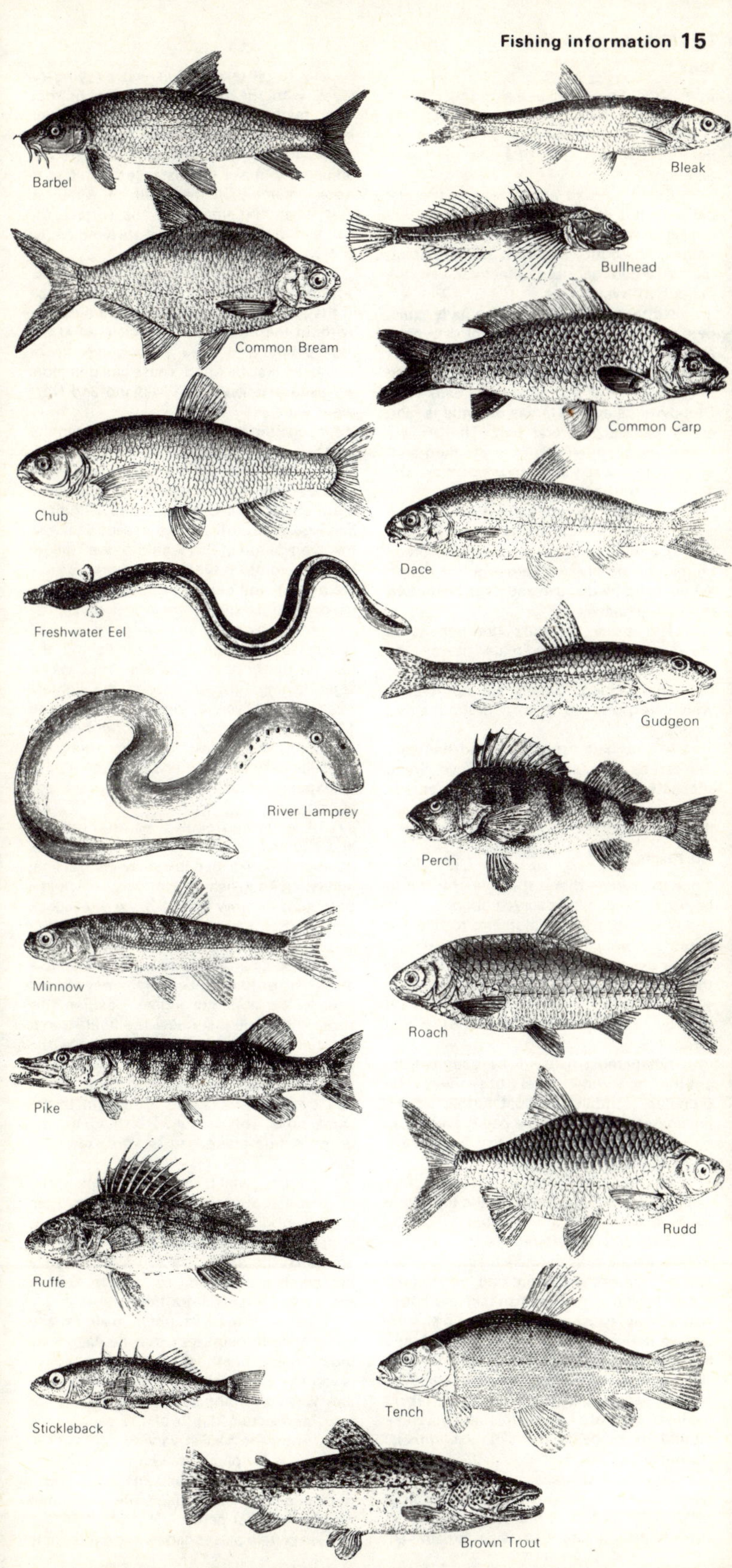
Barbel
Bleak
Bullhead
Common Bream
Common Carp
Chub
Dace
Freshwater Eel
Gudgeon
River Lamprey
Perch
Minnow
Roach
Pike
Rudd
Ruffe
Stickleback
Tench
Brown Trout

Bait

Baits should be small, and maggots, casters (maggot chrysalis), hempseed, wheat, tiny cubes of bread crust, or a small pinch of flake (the white crumb of a new loaf) may take fish.

But it pays to experiment with baits; bait which is effective on one occasion will not necessarily prove to be as effective the next. With slight variations, similar fishing methods can be used effectively on the majority of waterways.

Northern anglers who regularly compete in contests on canals use bloodworms as bait. They have become extremely skilful in using this tiny bait and often take fish on bloodworms when all other baits fail. Bloodworms are the larvae of a midge, and are a perfectly natural bait. The anglers gather the bloodworms from the mud and, apart from a wash in clean water, the baits are ready for use.

A popular groundbait which has had great success is known as 'black magic'! This is a mixture of garden peat and bread crumbs mixed dry and carried to the water. When dampened and mixed it can be thrown in in the usual way.

The basis of most groundbaits is bread, and many other materials may be added. But always avoid stodgy mixtures for canal fishing. Canals are not waters which respond to heavy groundbaiting tactics.

It is far better to use a cloud-bait, and this can be purchased ready for use. Some successful midland anglers wet their cloud-bait with milk instead of water to increase the cloud effect.

Methods

Once the swim–that is the area of water to be fished–has been decided upon, and the tackle set up, use the plummet to find the depth and adjust the float.

It usually pays to plumb the depth of the swim before fishing, but be cautious when doing so in clear waters. At times it may be best to find the depth by trial and error.

Often most fish will be caught from around mid-water level, but always be prepared to move the float further up the line in order to present the bait closer to the bottom, where the bigger fish are usually to be found.

At frequent intervals toss a few samples of the hook-bait into the top of the swim to keep the fish interested.

Fish vary in different swims, and on different waters, in the way they take a bait and this creates a different bite registration. It may be found that the fish take the hook-bait quickly, causing the float to dip sharply or dive under the surface. The strike should be made instantly, on the downward movement. On some canals the fish are even quicker–and perhaps gentler–not taking the float under at all, and in this case the strike should be made at the slightest unusual movement of the float.

Roach and dace abound in many lengths and although working the float tackle down with a flow of water takes most fish, better quality fish–also bream–are usually to be taken by fishing a laying-on style, with the bait lying on the bottom. This method can often be best when fishing areas where there is no flow at all.

This can be done with float tackle, adjusted to make the distance from float to hook greater than the depth of water, so that when the float is at the surface the bait and lower length of line are lying on the bottom.

The alternative method of fishing the bottom is by legering, the main difference in the methods being in the bite indication. Without the float a bite is registered at the rod-tip where, if need be, a quiver-tip or swing-tip may be fitted. These bite detectors are used extensively on Midland and Northern waters.

Legering is a method often used in the south, where in some southern canals barbel and chub are quite prolific. These species grow to good sizes in canal waters–chub up to 7lb and barbel up to 14lb have been taken–but these are exceptional and the average run of fish would be well below those weights. Nevertheless, both species are big fish and big baits and hooks may be used when fishing for them.

Many bigger than average fish–of all species–have been taken by fishing the bait on the bottom. Whatever the style of leger fishing, always choose the lightest possible lead weight, and position it some 12 to 18 inches up from the hook. There are no hard and fast rules governing the distance between lead and hook, so it pays to experiment to find the best to suit the conditions.

Anglers who regularly fish the northern, and midland canals invariably use tiny size 20 and 22 hooks, tied to a mere ¾lb b.s. line, and when float-fishing use a tiny quill float–porcupine or crow quill. A piece of peacock quill is useful because it can be cut with scissors to make it suit prevailing conditions.

Such small floats only need a couple of dust-shot to balance them correctly, and usually the midland anglers position this shot on the line just under the float so that the bait is presented naturally. Once the tackle has been cast out the bait falls slowly through the water along with hook-bait samples, which are thrown in at the same time. This is called 'fishing on the drop'. A fine cloud-bait is also used with this style.

Canals which have luxuriant weed growth harbour many small fish, which are preyed upon by perch. These move in shoals and invariably the perch in a shoal are much the same size. Usually the really big perch are solitary, so it pays to rove the canal and search for them.

Perch are to be caught from almost any canal and although they may be caught by most angling methods, the most effective is usually float-fishing. The fishing depth can vary according to conditions, time of year, and actual depth of the canal, so it pays to try the bait at varying depths. The usual baits for perch are worms, small live-baits (minnows etc) and maggots. Close by the wooden lock gates are very often good haunts for perch.

In certain places canals and rivers come

together and take on the characteristics of the river (i.e. with an increased flow) and different methods are needed. These places are often noted for splendid chub (and sometimes barbel) in addition to roach and other species. Trotting the stream is a popular and effective fishing style.

Weather

Weather conditions also have to be taken into consideration. Canals usually run through open country and catch the slightest breeze. Even a moderate wind will pull and bob the float, which in turn will agitate the baited hook. If bites are not forthcoming under such conditions then it may be best to remove the float and try a straight-forward leger arrangement.

When legering, the effects of the wind can be avoided by keeping the rod top down to within an inch or two of the water level—or even by sinking the rod-tip below the surface. Anglers in the north and mid-lands have devised a wind-shield for legering which protects the rod-tip from the wind and improves bite detection.

Nevertheless, in some circumstances a slight wind can be helpful because if a moderate breeze is blowing it will put a ripple on the water, and this can be of assistance in fishing in clear waters.

Where to fish

Most canals are narrow and this makes it possible to cast the tackle towards the far bank where fish have moved because they had been disturbed from the near bank. Disturbance will send the fish up or down-stream and often well away from the fishing area. So always approach the water quietly, and remember to move cautiously at all times. When making up the tackle to start fishing it is advisable to do so as far back from the water as possible to avoid scaring the fish. It pays to move slowly, to keep as far from the bank as possible, and to avoid clumping around in heavy rubber boots.

If there is cover along the bank—shrubs, bushes, tall reeds and clumps of yellow flag iris—the wise angler will make full use of it.

There are some canals which are not navigable, and these are generally weedy. At certain times in the season the surface of the water disappears under a green mantle of floating duckweed, which affords cover and security for the fish. It is possible to have the best sport by fishing in the pockets of clear water which are to be found.

Some canals have prolific growths of water lilies in places, and are particularly attractive for angling. They always look ideal haunts for tench, but they can also be rather difficult places from which to land good fish.

Tench are more or less evenly distributed throughout the canals and the best are found where weed growth is profuse. It may be best to fish small areas of clear water between the weeds. Groundbait can encourage tench to move out from the weed beds, and to feed once they are out. Sometimes it is an advantage to clear a swim by dragging out weeds or raking the bottom. This form of natural groundbaiting stirs the silt which clouds the water, and disturbs aquatic creatures on which the fish feed. Sometimes a tench is hooked within minutes of raking.

Bream seem to do well in canals and some fairly good fish up to 5lb may be taken. Some canals are noted for shoals of big bream, where it is possible to catch over 50lb of them at a session. Any deep pools or winding holes (shown as ∩ on map) are good places to try, particularly when fishing a canal for the first time.

Other places worth fishing are 'cattle drinks' regularly used by farm animals. These make useful places to fish for bream, roach and dace. The frequent use of these drinking holes colours the water, as the animals stir up the mud, and disturb various water creatures. The coloured water draws fish into the area—on the downstream side of the cattle drink when there is the slightest flow.

Pike are to be found in every canal in the country, and these grow big. They are predators, feeding on small fish (which gives a sure indication of the most effective baits.) Any small live fish presented on float tackle will take pike. The best places to fish are near weed beds and boats which have been moored in one place a long time.

Many of our canals are cut through pleasant and peaceful countryside, and this enables anglers to spend many delightful hours along the banks—and always with the chance of making a good catch.

As a general rule, never fish in locks on navigable canals, or anywhere that could obstruct the free passage of boats. Remember that you will inconvenience yourself as well as the boatman if you have to move in a hurry, or risk a broken line.

The BWB Fisheries Officer at Watford welcomes specific enquiries about fishing on BWB canals from individuals, associations and clubs. He will also supply the name and address of the current Secretary of each Angling Association.

Bridgwater & Taunton

This isolated canal represents a small part of a far more ambitious scheme–a ship canal linking Bristol to the long established Exeter Ship Canal–which was never executed. Instead, a more modest line was built from the River Parrett at Huntworth (just south of Bridgwater) to Taunton, and opened in 1827. Most of its revenue was drawn from traffic passing to and from the Chard and Grand Western Canals, which joined at Creech St Michael and Taunton respectively. In 1841 an extension was opened from Huntworth to Bridgwater, where the canal joined the River Parrett at Bridgwater Dock. In 1866 the navigation was sold to the Bristol & Exeter Railway Company, leaving its proprietors badly out of pocket. All barge traffic ceased in 1907. In 1940, at the behest of the War Office, the canal was turned into a line of defence against the possibility of enemy invasion, and pill boxes were erected at strategic points along it. The bridges were fixed and strengthened to carry WD vehicles. Ownership passed to the BWB in 1963. In 1965 the Somerset Inland Waterways Society was formed, and work continues towards the restoration of the canal. Bridgwater Dock has been purchased by Somerset County Council with recreational use in mind, and with the planned restoration of the barge lock off the River Parrett and the bascule bridge, plus the restoration of Newton Lock, will once more connect the canal to the sea.

Maximum dimensions
The canal is suitable for light craft only.

Mileage
TAUNTON Firepool Lock to
Creech St. Michael: 3
Durston: 6
North Newton: $7\frac{1}{4}$
BRIDGWATER Dock: $14\frac{1}{4}$
Total 6 locks

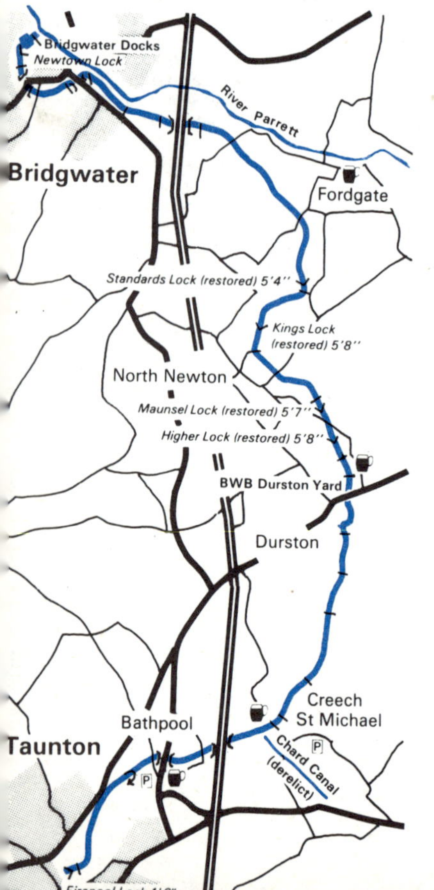

$14\frac{1}{4}$ miles

The Bridgwater & Taunton Canal runs through attractive rolling scenery, typical of rural Somerset. Although not at present navigable, it can be used by small boats and canoes over much of its length; the towpath offers a pleasant day's walk, the most simple way to enjoy the quiet pleasures of the canal. It begins at Firepool Lock, at a junction with the River Tone which was once navigable to its junction with the River Parrett at Bridgwater. It then curves past the railway station and passes under the Bristol Exeter line which follows the canal to Bridgwater. During the invasion scare of 1940, the swinging mechanism on many of the canal's bridges was destroyed so that the waterway could become a line of defence against German forces. The first of these low fixed bridges, now a major obstacle to restoration, is reached before Bathpool. The canal passes through flat pastureland, being crossed by the busy Bristol Exeter motorway before reaching Creech St Michael. The remains of the old Chard Canal can be seen to the west of the village, its embankment crossing the Tone flood plain to the south. Small agricultural hamlets flank the navigation, which is peaceful and rural until the motorway crosses it again before Bridgwater. The canal arcs round to the west of the town in a cutting, before reaching its junction with the Parrett Estuary at Bridgwater Dock. The river locks here have been replaced with concrete barriers, so there is now no access to the sea. The dock basins are sadly empty.

Taunton
Somerset. Pop 37,000. EC Thur. MD Tue/Sat. All services. A rich agricultural market town and route centre for the south west, retaining a well-knit and unspoilt appearance. Taunton Castle dates from the 12thC, and now houses the Somerset County Museum, *open weekdays.*

Bathpool
Somerset. PO, tel, stores, garage. A small canalside village devastated by the A38.

Chard Canal
Running $13\frac{1}{2}$ miles from Creech St Michael to Chard, the canal survived only 26 years, closing in 1868 due to railway competition. Little now remains.

Creech St Michael
Somerset. PO, tel, stores, garage. The old village and sturdy 13thC church are still there, surrounded by new houses.
Durston
Somerset. PO, tel, stores, garage. A scattered, not unattractive village along the A361.
North Newton
Somerset. PO, tel, stores, garage. An irregular farming village, with houses of all periods and an eccentric looking church. The Alfred Jewel, the oldest surviving crown jewel was found here in 1693. Those who walk the extra $1\frac{1}{2}$ miles to North Petherton will be rewarded with the sight of a 109ft 15thC church tower, one of the most richly decorated in Somerset.
Fordgate
Somerset. Tel. Farming village which stretches from the canal to the deep banks of the River Parrett.
Bridgwater
Somerset. Pop 26,700. EC Thur. MD Wed. All services. Little of the medieval town is left, due to a destructive Civil War siege, but here and there are signs of 18thC wealth, especially Castle Street with its handsome houses. Eclipsed as a port by Bristol, the old quay is attractive–in the Shipbroker's Office is a Fortin barometer to consult before sailing. The 19thC dock is still intact, but disused–winches, bollards and broken cranes stand idle. The Admiral Blake Museum contains Blake relics and local items, *open weekdays, closed Tues aft.*
Grand Western Canal
Originally part of a scheme to link the English and Bristol Channels, the Grand Western Canal was to run from Taunton to Exeter, with branches to Tiverton and Cullompton. It was never completed, a financial disaster from the start because of railway competition. The attractive Tiverton branch is still in water and used extensively by small craft and two horse-drawn trip boats (for information ring Tiverton 3345).

BOATYARDS & BWB

BWB Bathpool Taunton (73576).

PUBS

Castle Hotel Taunton (2671). Food. Booking essential.
Bathpool Inn Bathpool. Food, camping and caravan site.
Bell Inn Creech St. Michael.
New Inn Creech St. Michael.
Railway Hotel Durston.
Harvest Moon North Newton.
Thatchers Arms Fordgate. Overlooking the River Parrett.

The Grand Western Canal at Sampford Peverell. *Derek Pratt.*

Grand Union Canal

The Grand Union comprises at least 8 separate canals, linking London with Birmingham, Leicester and Nottingham. Once owned and operated by separate companies, they made up the spine of southern England's transport system until the advent of the railways.

The original part was the Grand Junction Canal, constructed at the turn of the 18thC to provide a short cut between Brentford and Braunston, cutting 60 miles off the journey from the Midlands to London. Having wide locks and numerous branches to important towns, it soon became busy and popular. If the other companies had followed the Grand Junction's example, and widened their canals, the history of English canals might have turned out very different.

Meanwhile in London, in 1812, the Regent's Canal Company was formed to cut a new canal round London to Limehouse. This proved highly successful and 10 years later the Hertford Union was built for connection with the River Lee.

The Regent's Canal Company later acquired the Grand Junction and others. The whole system was integrated as the Grand Union Canal Company in 1929, and a massive programme of modernisation was launched in 1932, aided by the Government. Widening locks, piling and dredging work took place but the grant ran out before it was finished. The Grand Union could only decline commercially, but it remains today a vital part of the inland cruising network.

Maximum dimensions

Regents Canal
Length: 72', Beam: 14' 6"
Headroom: 9'

Brentford and Paddington to Birmingham (Camp Hill Top Lock)
Length: 72', Beam: 12' 6"
Headroom: 7' 11"

Norton Junction to Foxton Junction
Length: 72', Beam: 7'
Headroom: 7' 6"

Market Harborough to Leicester
Length: 72', Beam: 10'
Headroom: 7'

Aylesbury and Northampton Arms
Length: 72', Beam: 7'
Headroom: 7'

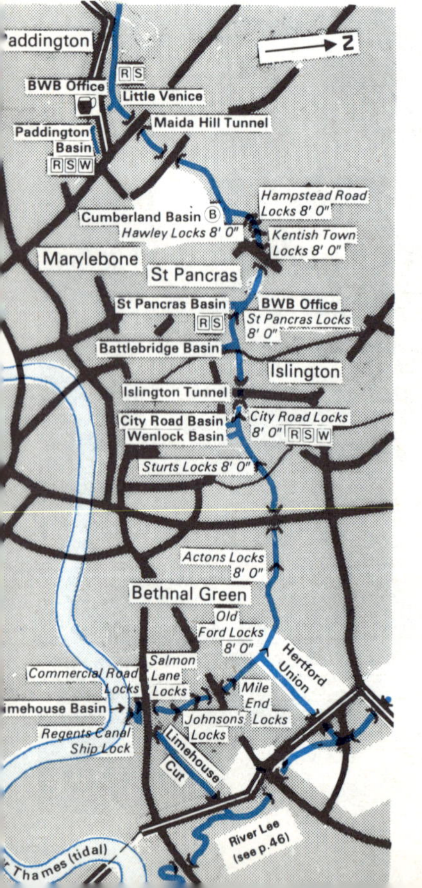

9 miles

In the Greater London area, most specific information relates directly to the canal. However some canalside and nearby pubs and restaurants are included. For places and features of interest see 'Nicholson's London Guide'.

The Regent's Canal begins at Limehouse Basin in London's dockland and climbs up round central London to end at Little Venice in Paddington. It supports a small trade, mostly in timber, but is remarkably private and peaceful.

The Regent's Canal ship lock between the Thames and Limehouse Basin (also the entrance to the River Lee navigation) is only opened during the three hours preceding every high water. Any queries should be put to the Section office (01-790 3444).

The locks on the Regent's Canal, all barge-sized, are *open at all times*. The Canal Office at Little Venice (01-286 6101) will give information and assistance. It is advisable to inform this office (or the Dock-master's) when intending to use the canals in London.

The Hertford Union Canal (Duckett's), is a useful short cut between the Regent's Canal and the Lee Navigation. Its three locks may only be operated by lock-keepers. Ring the Section Office at 01-790 3444.

To the left of Little Venice, the vast Paddington Basin makes an excellent 24hr mooring site, being close to the West End of London. To the right is the Paddington Arm of the former Grand Junction Canal.

Limehouse Basin
Limehouse. Terminus of the Regent's Canal and the Lee Navigation. Once known as the Regent's Canal Dock. Now almost empty except for lighters passing through.

Victoria Park
Hackney. Almost 300 acres of parkland designed by James Pennthorne, a protégé of Nash, and laid between 1842 and 1845.

Islington Tunnel
960 yards. Open in 1816. In 1826 a towing boat was introduced which pulled itself to and fro along a chain laid on the

canal bed. This system remained until the 1930's.

Regent's Park
Originally part of Henry VIII's great hunting forest in the 16thC. The park is surrounded by handsome Regency terraces and gateways.

London Zoo
Regent's Park. One of the largest in the world. The zoo was originally laid out in 1827 and many famous architects have designed special animal houses.

Cumberland Basin
A small basin by the zoo which used to form the junction of the Regent's Canal main line with a branch that led off to Cumberland Market near Euston Station. Now full of moored boats, it also has a floating restaurant.

Lords Cricket Ground
St John's Wood rd NW8. (01-289 1615). Ground of the MCC. Test match in *Jun*.

Canalside Walk
Between Lisson Grove (east end of Maida Hill Tunnel) and Regent's Park Zoo. Two miles of the canal towpath are open as a charming public walk. Walk on to Camden Lock and visit the craft shops and weekend market.

The Pirate Castle
Exotic brick building housing a boat club for local children.

Little Venice
On the junction of the Regent's and Grand Junction Canals, famous for elegant houses and colourful boats. Still known as Paddington Stop by boatmen.

BOATYARDS & BWB

Ⓑ **BWB Canal Office** Delamere terrace W2. (01-286 6101). R S W Moorings, Waterbus service, general information.

St Pancras Basin Camley st NW1. R S Permanent moorings, slipway, chandlery. Apply to St Pancras Yacht Club, 01-278 2805.

Ⓑ **Turner Marinas** 57 Fitzroy rd NW1. (01-722 9806) R W Slipway, chandlery, toilets, engine repairs. Moorings (at Little Venice, Cumberland Basin and Lisson Grove).

CRUISES

BWB Zoo Waterbuses Delamere terrace W2. (01-286 6101). Half-hour trip through Regent's Park into the Zoo.

Jason's Trip 60 Blomfield rd W9. (01-286 3428). A traditional canal narrow boat leaves from the Canaletto Gallery *daily except Monday*, for a 1½hr trip. Must book in advance.

Jenny Wren Cruises 250 Camden High st NW1. (01-485 6210). Cruising restaurant. 1½ hr and longer narrow boat trips.

PUBS & RESTAURANTS

Freemason Salmon lane E14.

Vulcan Salmon lane E14.

Good Friends restaurant, 139 Salmon lane E14. (01-987 5541). Famous Chinese food.

Warwick Castle Warwick place W9. Little Venice. Sandwiches.

Didier's Warwick place W9. (01-286 7484). French restaurant. *Closed Sun*.

Bridge House Hotel Delamere terrace W2. Little Venice. Bar billiards.

Leisure Tyme 374 Edgware rd, W2. (01-402 9994). Cruising restaurant based at Little Venice. English food. Individuals and parties catered for. *Departs daily 19.30*. Must book.

Barque & Bite Prince Albert rd NW1. (01-485 8137). Converted floating barge at Cumberland Basin. French restaurant.

Byron Restaurant 46 Inverness st NW1. (01-267 4682). Genuine Greek food. *Closed Sun L.*

Fair Lady Camden Lock, Commercial place, Chalk Farm rd NW1. (01-485 4433). Cruising restaurant. English food. Individuals and parties catered for. Departs *Mon-Sat 19.30, Sun 12.30*. Must book.

Narrow Boat 119 St Peter st, Islington. Canalside. Food.

Island Queen 87 Noel rd, Islington. (01-226 5507). Near City rd Basin.

Carrier's 2 Camden passage, Islington. (01-226 5353). Famous restaurant. *Closed Sun.*

Portofino 39 Camden passage, Islington. (01-226 0884). Italian restaurant. *Closed Sun.*

Constitution 42 St Pancras way. Canalside.

Au Bois St Jean 122 St John's Wood High st. (01-586 1022). French provincial restaurant. *Closed Sun.*

Hanwell locks

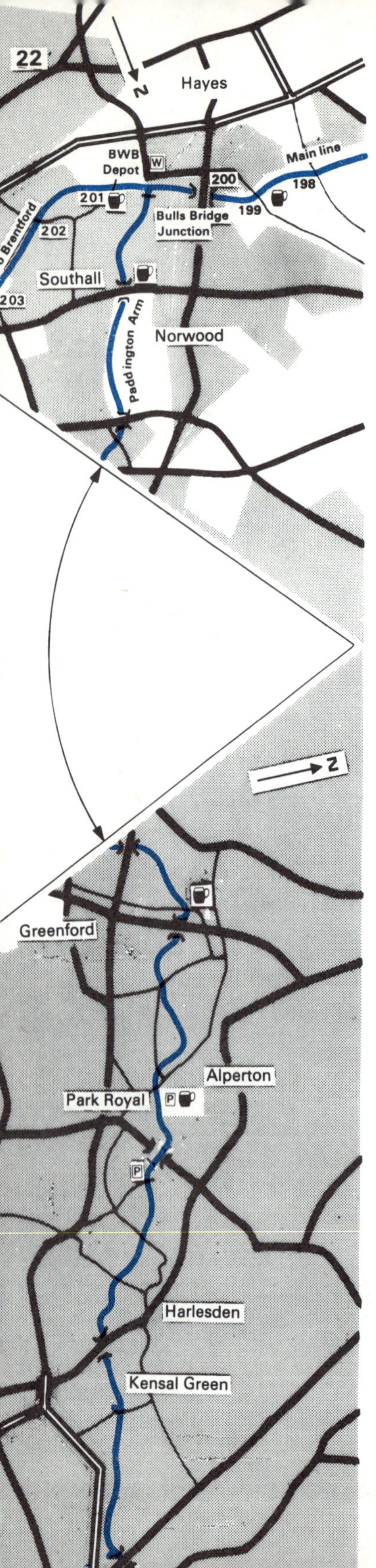

Grand Union

West London

13 miles

The Paddington Arm carries no trade now. The stretch of canal through suburban Middlesex is remarkable for the large number of private arms and basins which once served gasworks, factories and warehouses. Another feature of the Arm is the 'horse dips' or steps down into the water from the towpath, built to facilitate the removal of horses which fell into the 'cut'. The Paddington Arm joins the Grand Union Main Line at Bull's Bridge Junction where maintenance boats are built and repaired in a large BWB depot. Turning left leads to Brentford and the Thames, right to Birmingham and the North.

Kensal Green Cemetery
Opened in 1833. Water gates set in the wall indicate that once coffins for burial could be brought up by barge. Many famous people are buried here.
Wormwood Scrubs
Expanse of open space and the famous prison.
St Mary Magdalene
Alongside the canal W of Little Venice. Built by Street, 1868-78. Tall Gothic spire and richly decorated crypt.
Southall
Middx. EC Wed. Extensive modern shopping centre.
Martinware Pottery Collection
Southall Public Library, Osterley Park rd. Collection of Martinware, including birds, face mugs and grotesqueries. 'Art nouveau'. *Closed Sun.*
Hayes & Harlington
Middx. EC Wed. Much industralised area. Good for shops and pubs.
Hayes & Harlington Museum Golden crescent. Local interest. *Closed Wed afternoon, Sun.*

BOATYARDS & BWB

BWB Bull's Bridge Depot Bull's Bridge. Hayes rd, Southall. (01-573 2368). D (emergency only). *Open Mon–Fri.*
Ⓑ **Porta Bella Dock** Corner of Ladbroke grove and Kensal rd, W10. (01-960 5456). W A new marina/market/restaurant complex. Regular boat trips from here.

PUBS & RESTAURANTS

- ✕ **Black Horse** Black Horse bridge, Greenford. Canalside. Food, garden.
- **Pleasure Boat** Bridgewater rd, Alperton. Canalside. Food.
- **Grand Junction Arms** Acton Lane, Harlesden. Canalside.
- **Foresters Arms** West Drayton. (80 yds from bridge 195). Food.
- ✕ **Blue Anchor** Hayes. Canalside, at bridge 199. Food.
- **Grand Junction Arms** Southall. (By bridge 201). Canalside. Food.
- **Hambrough Tavern** Southall. Canalside, at A4020 bridge.

Uxbridge

Brentford section 6 miles, Bull's Bridge to Denham 7 miles.

The main line left of Bull's Bridge Junction ends at the Thames in Brentford. Norwood Top Lock is padlocked every night *(17.00 winter, 20.30 summer)*. Brentford and Thames Locks are opened for 2-2½ hours either side of every high water. Enquiries 01-560 8941.
Right from Bull's Bridge the main line bends towards Cowley Lock where it starts climbing towards the Chilterns-- up the Colne Valley and across Harefield Moor where there is a large mooring site in a flooded gravel pit linked to the canal.

Osterley House
Isleworth. (01-560 3918). Adam interior. Fine tapestries and carpets.
Boston Manor House
Boston Manor rd, Brentford. (01-560 3485). Tudor, Jacobean.
British Piano Museum
High st, Brentford. (01-560 8108).
Syon House
Brentford. (01-560 3225). Adam interior, period furniture, paintings. Gardening Centre in grounds.
Syon Park Gardening Centre
Park rd, Brentford. (01-560 0881). Capability Brown landscape.
Kew Gardens
Kew. (01-940 1171). Thousands of rare outdoor and hothouse plants. Kew Palace.
Yiewsley & West Drayton
Middx. Pop 23,720. EC Wed. All services.
Uxbridge
Middx. Pop 63,940. EC Wed. All services.
Narrowboat 'Pisces' Ex-working canal boat now owned and operated from Cowley Lock. Can be hired from the Council's Education Department. (Uxbridge 38232).
Langley
Bucks. Pop 3420. EC Wed. All services.
Denham
Bucks. Pop 7700. EC Wed. All services.
See church in old village (Doom painting of 1460), Denham Court and Denham Place.

BOATYARDS & BWB

Ⓑ **BWB Norwood Yard** Norwood Top Lock. (01-574 1220). R S W

Ⓑ **Grand Union Cruisers** Packet Boat lane, Cowley Peachey. (West Drayton 40325). R S W D Pump-out. Repairs, hire narrow boats. Mooring, chandlery, toilets, winter storage. Wine bar and shop.

Ⓑ **Uxbridge Boat Centre** Uxbridge Wharf, Waterloo rd (Uxbridge 52019). R S W D Repairs, servicing, chandlery, installations, DIY facilities, undercover storage, slipway, toilets. *Closed Mon.*

Ⓑ **Denham Yacht Station** Uxbridge (39811). R W P D Slipway, chandlery, boat sales and repairs, gas, toilets, winter storage. Club house, facilities, temporary moorings and restaurant.

PUBS & RESTAURANTS

Old Oak Tree Southall (at bridge 202). Canalside. Food. Near grocery, tel.

Lamb Norwood (at bridge 203). Canalside. Near PO, shops.

Fox Green lane, Hanwell Locks. Food.

Northumberland Arms near Brentford Locks.

Swan and Bottle 98 High st, Uxbridge (43047). Canalside near bridge 185.

General Elliott St John's rd, Uxbridge (37385). Canalside near bridge 186.

Shovel Cowley lock, Uxbridge (33121). Canalside. Food.

Anchor West Drayton. Canalside, north of bridge 192.

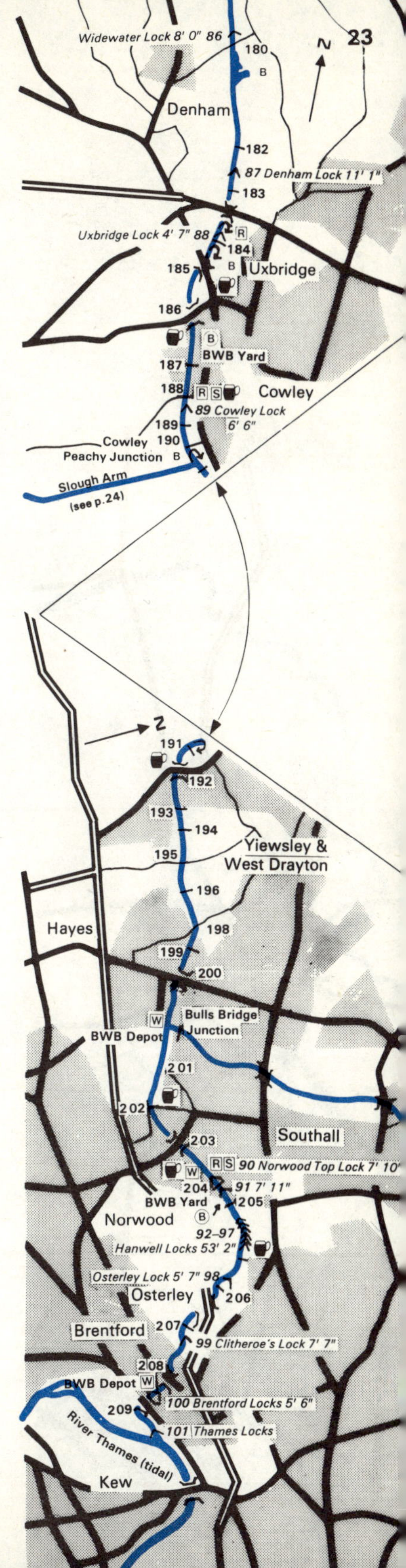

Slough

5 miles

Between Cowley Peachey Junction and Slough is the five mile lock-free Slough Arm. Built as late as 1883 (the last canal to be built in Britain apart from the Manchester Ship Canal) it supports no trade, but there is a useful boatyard near Iver.

Iver
Bucks. Pop 11,300. EC Wed. All services. The church has a Saxon nave with Roman bricks visible in the walls, Norman arches, medieval art and Tudor monuments. The 700-year-old tower owes its height to the 15thC bell chamber.
Old Slade Nature Reserve
1m south of Iver station. Gravel pit taken over by the Berkshire, Buckinghamshire and Oxfordshire Naturalists' Trust and now a wealth of bird and animal life.
Iver Grove
Shredding Green, Iver (north of the Boatyard). A fine mansion built by Sir John Vanbrugh in 1724. Not open to the public.
Slough
Bucks. Pop 85,690. EC Wed. MD Tue. All services. The largest town in Buckinghamshire. A new town with a wide range of light industries and a great concern for road safety. St Mary's church, completed in 1876, has stained glass by Kempe and Alfred J. Wolmark.

BOATYARDS & BWB

Ⓑ **High line Yachting** Mansion lane, Iver. (651496). R S W D Moorings, repairs, slipway, hire cruisers, boat building, gas, chandlery, toilets, showers, winter storage.

PUBS & RESTAURANTS

Swan High st, Iver. Food *(except weekends)*.
Red Lion Shredding green, Iver. Food.
Paddington Packet Boat Cowley Peachey. Food.
Prince of Wales Commercial rd, Slough. (21530). Food.

Grand Union

Rickmansworth

13 miles

From Widewater Lock the canal continues north up the Colne Valley. At Batchworth, northbound boatmen should take the right hand lock to stay on the Grand Union (the other leads a short distance up the River Chess). The canal climbs through Cassiobury Park towards Kings Langley. There are several wide stretches. Do not attempt to turn without ascertaining the depth.

Harefield
Middx. PO, tel, stores. The church is like a small museum. Norman masonry, box pews, 16thC screen, 19thC Gothic gallery and many other features.

Copper Mill
Once a paper mill it turned to making copper sheets for the bottom of boats after the canal was built. South of here is Troy Cut (unnavigable), which leads to the ancient Troy Mill.

Springwell and Stocker's Locks
This stretch is of interest to naturalists for its great variety of plants.

Rickmansworth
Herts. Pop 28,540. EC Wed. All services. Many worthwhile buildings.

Moor Park Mansion House
1m SE of canal. Fine Palladian house with superb interior decorations. *Open Mon afternoons (other days by appointment). Closed bank hols.*

Rickmansworth Aquadrome
Bury & Batchworth Lakes. Facilities for all types of water sports. *Open daily.* Aqua show held *every Whit Mon.*

Croxley Green
Herts. All services. Papermill by lock 79, home of 'Croxley Script'.

Cassiobury Park
190 acres. Avenue of limes planted in 1672. Ornamental stone bridge. Watford's carnival is held here *every Whitsun.*

Hunton Bridge
Herts. PO, tel, stores. Peaceful canalside village with a spired church.

Aldenham Reservoir
Canal feeder reservoir near Elstree. Angling facilities available. Enquiries to Elstree 1158.

Abbots Langley
Herts. Pop 18,150. EC Wed. All services. The church of St Lawrence dates from the 12thC.

Kings Langley
Herts. Pop 5000. EC Wed. All services. The tomb of Edmund de Langley, brother of the Black Prince, lies in the Norman Church of All Saints.

BOATYARDS & BWB

Ⓑ **Cassio Bridge Marina** Cassio Bridge, Watford (34113). R S W Slipway, gas, mooring, chandlery, toilets, provisions, storage. *Closed Sun in winter.*

CRUISES

Arcturus Cruisers Cassio Wharf, Watford. (Enquiries Guildford 63989). Narrow boat cruises for parties of up to 54. Public trips *Sun afternoon Easter to Oct.* from lock 77

PUBS & RESTAURANTS

Black Jack's Mill Restaurant. Canalside. (Harefield 3120).

Fisheries Copper Mill lock, Harefield. (3180). Canalside. Food.

Halfway House near Widewater lock. Food.

New Halfway House near Cassio Bridge (169)

Batchworth Arms near Batchworth lock. Food.

White Bear near Batchworth lock. Lunches Mon-Fri. Bar billiards.

Dog & Partridge Old Mill rd, Hunton Bridge. (Kings Langley 65881).

Lamb near Kings Langley lock. Food.

King's Head Hunton Bridge. (Kings Langley 62307). Food, except Sun.

Unicorn Gallows hill. Hunton Bridge. Food. Quaint 450-year-old pub.

150
Hemel Hempstead
Boxmoor Lock 7' 1" 64
151
Apsley
BWB Yard
25
65–67 Apsley Locks 16' 0"
154
68–69 Nash Mills Locks 12' 2"
N
157
69A Kings Langley Lock 8' 9"
158
Kings Langley
Abbots Langley
70 5' 2"
159
N
71 6' 11"
Hunton Bridge
162
72–73 Hunton Bridge Locks 11' 2"
Lady Capel's Lock 5' 4" 74
163
164
165
166
75–76
Cassiobury Park Locks 10' 0"
Watford Lock 9' 4" 77
167
168
Cassio Bridge Lock 9' 0" 78
Watford
169
79 Common Moor Lock 9' 5"
170
Rickmansworth
80 Lot Mead Lock 6' 3"
81 Batchworth Lock 6' 8"
173
Batchworth
82 Stocker's Lock 5' 2"
175
176
83 Springwell Lock 7' 11"
84 Copper Mill Lock 5' 10"
177
85 Black Jack's Lock 3' 8"
178
Harefield
179
86 Widewater Lock 8' 0"
180
182

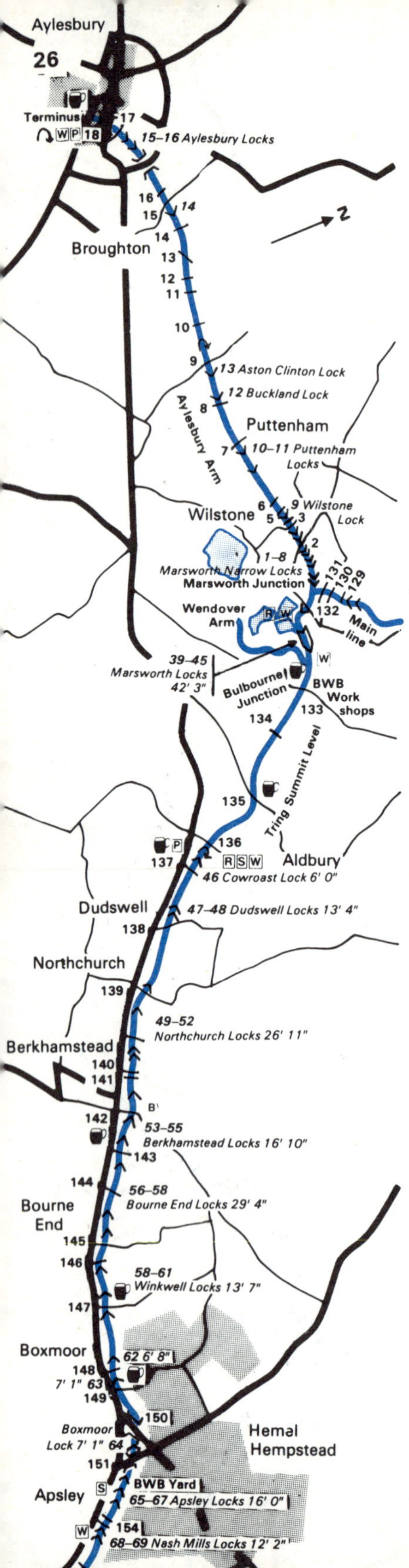

Marsworth

Hemel to Marsworth 10 miles. Aylesbury Arm $6\frac{3}{4}$ miles

Climbing past Hemel Hempstead the canal passes close to the A41 (good for petrol stations, shops and pubs) and enters Berkhamsted, the northern limit of the Grand Union as a barge canal. Climbing on towards the Chilterns, the summit level is reached at Cowroast Lock. At Bulbourne Junction, the Wendover Arm is navigable for small boats to Little Tring and the Tringford pumping station (the stop plank may be removed for access to this arm), and at Marsworth Junction the Aylesbury Arm starts to fall westwards. Totally isolated and remote, its locks are only 7 feet wide. The bridges – particularly bridge 18 – are also extremely narrow. Aylesbury has no actual boatyard but there are moorings, water and fuel near the basin.

Hemel Hempstead
Herts. Pop 68,000. EC Wed. MD Thu/Fri/Sat. All services. Excellent shops.
Piccotts End Medieval Murals 138
Piccotts End. 14thC wall paintings.
Berkhamsted
Herts. Pop 15,040. EC Wed. MD Sat. All services. Church of St Peter has work from practically every period. Ruins of Norman castle. Intact 17thC almshouses.
Northchurch
Herts. Pop 1170. EC Wed. PO, tel, stores. Flint church with some Saxon work and 19thC stained glass.
Aldbury
Herts. PO, tel, stores. Church of St John the Baptist dates from 13thC. Monument to third Duke of Bridgewater, the canal pioneer.
Aldbury Common
E of bridge 135 past Tring Station. Acres of open land.
Bulbourne
Herts. Tel. BWB workshops where craftsmen still make wooden lock gates. 19thC canal architecture. Near Stephenson's railway cutting.
Marsworth
Bucks. Pop 570. PO, tel, stores, garage. Icknield Way (Roman road), passes the village.
Tringford Pumping Station
Terminus of Wendover Arm. Water is fed into the Tring summit level.
Tring Reservoirs
S of Startop's End (bridge 132). National nature reserve.
Wilstone
Herts. PO, tel, stores.
Aylesbury
Bucks. Pop 36,500. EC Thur. MD Wed/Sat. All services. Busy market town with expanding industries. Attractive squares in town centre. 13thC church. Some Georgian buildings.
Buckinghamshire County Museum
Church st, Aylesbury (2158). Mainly local interest.
Hartwell House
$1\frac{1}{2}$m SW of Aylesbury. Jacobean. Ruined Gothic revival church. *Open May–July Weds & Bank hol. weekend. (Garden only Sept Wed).*

BOATYARDS & BWB

Ⓑ **BWB Apsley Yard** Ebberns rd, Apsley. (Hemel Hempstead 56910). R W
Ⓑ **Bridgewater Boats** Castle Wharf, Berkhamsted (3615) D Pump-out, gas. Hire narrow boats. Slipway, toilets, emergency repairs. *Open Mar–Oct.*

CRUISES

Grebe Canal Cruises Kingslyn, Munday Dene, Marlow, Bucks. (Marlow 72500). Day trips *Jul and Aug*; scheduled service *Bank hols*, private charter all year. Also operate *summer* Milton Keynes waterbus from The Three Locks, Soulbury.

PUBS & RESTAURANTS

Three Horseshoes Winkwell, Boxmoor. Canalside. Food.
Fishery Inn Fishery rd, Boxmoor. Canalside. (Hemel Hempstead 3539). Food.
Chez Danali 16 High st, Hemel Hempstead. (3752). Restaurant.
Old Kings Arms High st, Hemel Hempstead. (55348). English & Chinese.
White Hart High st, Hemel Hempstead. Food.
Cowroast opposite Cowroast lock. Restaurant meals.
George & Dragon Northchurch. Food.
Crystal Palace near Berkhamsted station. Canalside.
Boat Gravel path, Berkhamsted. Canalside. Food at lunchtime.
Rising Sun George st, Berkhamsted. Canalside at lock 55. Food.
Hung On 79 High st, Berkhamsted. (3186). Restaurant (Chinese).
Bull Inn High st, Berkhamsted, below lock 55. Calor gas available. Food.
Red Lion Marsworth, near bridge 130.
White Lion Marsworth. Canalside, at bridge 132. Food, water, refuse.
Lock & Quay Bulbourne. Canalside, at bridge 133. Food. R
Queens Head Marsworth, near bridge 132.
Royal Hotel Tring station. (Tring 2169). Lunches and dinners daily.
Bell Inn Aston Clinton. (252). 1m SE bridge 9. Famous restaurant.
Buckingham Arms Wilstone.
Half Moon Wilstone.
Bell Hotel Market square, Aylesbury. (2141). Restaurant.
Ship Aylesbury basin. Canalside.
Kings Head Market square, Aylesbury. (5158)., Restaurant owned by the National Trust. 15thC.

Leighton Buzzard

17 miles

Northwards from Marsworth the canal falls away from Dunstable Downs and the Chilterns towards Leighton Buzzard and Linsdale, passing between them, and meanders along the Ouzel Valley, skirting Bletchley, to Woolstone. The towpath is badly eroded between Simpson and Woughton.

Ivinghoe
Bucks. 1m E of bridge 123 or 126. Pop 810. EC Wed. PO, tel, stores, garage. Large 13thC and 14thC church with crossing tower and Jacobean pulpit. Pitstone Green Mill (ancient monument) is $\frac{1}{4}$m S of the village.

Iron Age Hill Fort
1m NE of Ivinghoe, on top of Beacon Hill. Triangular hill fort with bowl barrow, possibly Bronze Age. Tumuli.

Cheddington
Bucks. 1m N of bridge 126. Pop 1000. EC Thur. All services. The church has a richly carved Jacobean pulpit.

Mentmore Towers
1$\frac{1}{2}$m W of Horton Lock. Tudor style stone mansion built in the 1850's by Sir Joseph Paxton for the Rothschild family. Contents auctioned 1977 for £6 million.

Whipsnade White Lion
Dunstable Downs, visible from the canal around Slapton and Cheddington. The lion, cut in 1935 is over 480ft long.

Slapton
Bucks. Pop 240. EC Thur, PO, tel, stores. Perpendicular church with 15thC and 16thC brasses.

Grove
Bucks. Lock, lock cottage, tiny church and 14thC chapel with a later bell turret.

Leighton Buzzard
Beds. Pop 17,820. EC Thur. All services. Superb church. 17thC and 18thC houses

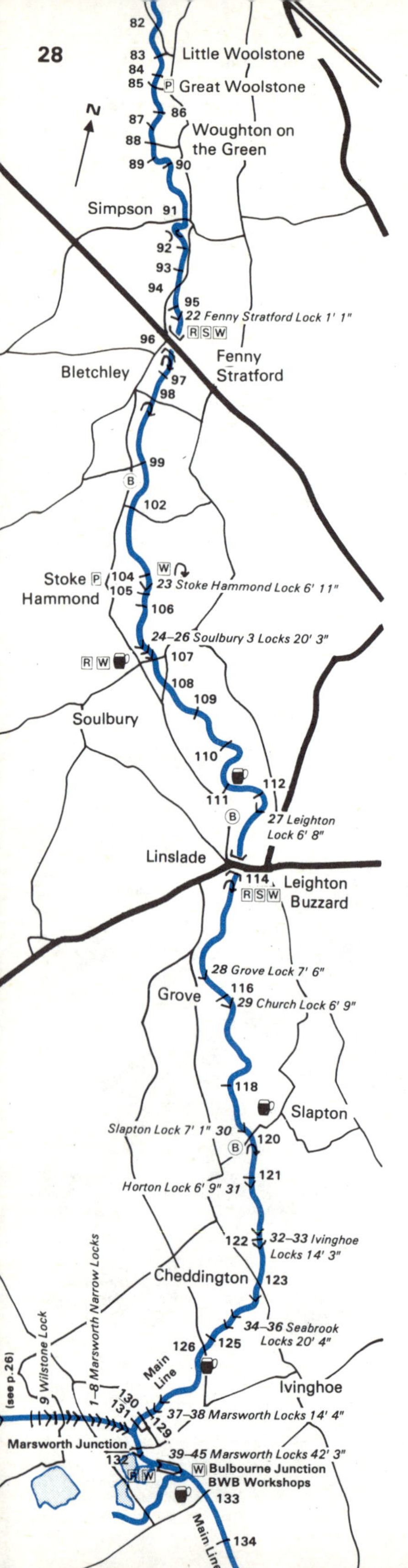

Leighton Buzzard (cont)

and half-timbered cottages in the streets leading to the 600-year-old Market Cross. Some fine 19thC buildings, and 17thC almshouses in North street.

All Saint's Parish Church
Dates from 1288. 191ft tower and spire, 15thC wooden roof. Ancient sanctus bell, 13thC font, misericordes, brasses and medieval lectern. Medieval graffiti.

Linslade
Bucks. Pop 2370. All services. Note the battlements of the church to the north of the canal. The font and parts of the structures date from the 12thC.

Ascott House
2m W of Linslade. Timber-framed, built in 1606. Paintings, French and Chippendale furniture, oriental porcelain. Rare trees in grounds.

Soulbury
Bucks. 1m W of the Three Locks. Pop 460. PO, tel, stores. Church with monument by Grinling Gibbons, 1690. To the south is 17thC Liscombe House.

Stoke Hammond
Bucks. Pop 420. EC Sat. PO, tel, stores, garage. The church, with its squat tower, has a 14thC font.

Fenny Stratford
Bucks. PO, tel, stores, garage, station. Red brick church, 1724-30; early example of Gothic revival.

Woburn Abbey
5m E of Fenny Stratford. 18thC mansion. State apartments, French and English 18thC silver, paintings. Deer forest, wild animal park, bird sanctuary, antique market. *Open daily.*

Bletchley
Bucks. Pop 23,400. EC Wed. MD Thur/Sat. All services. Being swallowed up by the new city of Milton Keynes. A small part of 12thC St Mary's church remains.

Simpson
Bucks. PO, tel, stores. Church mainly 14thC; note the wooden roof, and monument by John Bacon (1789).

Woughton on the Green
Bucks. Pop 160. PO, tel, stores. Houses of all periods. Random but harmonious.

Little Woolstone
Bucks. Tiny hamlet: a pub and a garage. Great Woolstone is even smaller.

BOATYARDS & BWB

Ⓑ **The Wyvern Shipping Co** Rothschild rd, Lynslade, Leighton Buzzard (372 355). W D Boat hire, gas, dry dock, boat building, mooring, toilets, trip boat for charter.

Ⓑ **Autrant Waterway Services** Little Billington, Leighton Buzzard (73552). Pump-out (not Wed). R S W D Hire craft, gas, boat and engine repairs.

PUBS & RESTAURANTS

Carpenters Arms Slapton.
✕ **Kings Head** Ivinghoe. (Cheddington 264 & 388). Restaurant.
Old Swan High st, Cheddington. (343).
Three Horseshoes Cheddington.
Stag Inn Mentmore. (Cheddington 423).
Duke of Wellington S of bridge 126.
Globe Inn Globe lane, Linsdale. (Leighton Buzzard 3338). Canalside, near bridge 111. Food.
✕ **Mayflower Grill** 4 High st, Leighton Buzzard. Restaurant. *EC Thur.*
Dolphin Stoke Hammond. Food.
✕ **Three Locks** Stoke Hammond. (Soulbury 243). Canalside. Garden, water, refuse disposal.
✕ **Barge Inn** Little Woolstone. Food.
✕ **Old Swan** Woughton on the Green. Food.
Plough Simpson.
Red Lion Fenny Stratford lock, Bletchley. (2317). Canalside R W Food, garden, camping, groceries.
Bridge Fenny Stratford. Canalside, at A5 bridge. Food.

Grand Union

Stoke Bruerne

16 miles

The canal continues north west following the Ouse Valley, crossing the river at the Wolverton Aqueduct. At Great Linford there is a winding hole that marks the junction with the old Newport Pagnell branch, many years closed. Another long abandoned branch, the Buckingham Arm, part of which is now a nature reserve, can be seen at Cosgrove Lock. Beyond Grafton Regis, by the junction of the canal and the River Tove, is a winding hole. The canal now starts the 7-lock climb to Stoke Bruerne, via wide single locks. After Bruerne Top Lock the level remains unchanged for several miles. A deep cutting leads to Blisworth Tunnel, the second longest in Britain still navigable. At Gayton Junction the Northampton Arm branches away north east.

Willen
Bucks. ½m E of bridge 81. PO box, tel. Wren church built in 1679 by Robert Hooke. A city church alone in empty fields. Tall nave and tower. The interior fittings are original.

Great Linford
Bucks. Pop 280. PO, tel, stores. Unchanged 18thC village with 14thC church containing Georgian box pews and pulpit, and 19thC stained glass. 17thC almshouses.

New Bradwell
Bucks. PO, tel, stores. Victorian railway town. The church by Street, 1858, has interesting stained glass. Bird observatory.

Wolverton
Bucks. Pop 13,600. EC Wed. MD Fri. All services. The large Norman style church in Old Wolverton was built in 1815. The Old Vicarage by the church, built in 1729, has a handsome portal.

Great Ouse Aqueduct
Iron trunk aqueduct, a square cast iron trough carried on stone pillars. Built in 1811, it replaced a brick structure that collapsed in 1808. This in turn had replaced 9 locks which enabled the Ouse to be crossed on the level, a system abandoned because of the danger of floods.

Cosgrove
Northants. Pop 400. EC Wed. PO, tel, stores. The best parts are by the canal. See the pedestrian tunnel and Gothic style stone bridge. Also Cosgrove Hall (Georgian), by the lock.

Castlethorpe
Bucks. Pop 460. PO, tel, stores. Thatched houses around a green, 1m NE of Castlethorpe Wharf. Parts of the church date back to 1200. N of the church is the site of a castle.

Yardley Gobion
Northants. Pop 580. EC Wed. PO, tel, stores. Thatch and stone village. The church was built in 1864.

Grafton Regis
Northants. Pop 170. EC Sat. PO, tel, stores. Stone village with strong manorial atmosphere. The church, near the canal, is mostly 13thC and 14thC, but contains a Norman font.

Stoke Bruerne
Northants. Pop 270. EC Sat. PO, tel, stores. Built mostly of Blisworth stone. The warehouses and cottages along the wharf have become a canal centre, encouraged by the presence of the Waterways Museum. Pleasure trips to Blisworth tunnel mouth (*summer*). Perpendicular church with Norman tower.

Waterways Museum Stoke Bruerne. (Roade 862229). Unique collection that brings to life the rich history of over 200 years of canals. Museum shop selling canal literature, maps, souvenirs, etc. *Open daily (except Xmas, Boxing Day and winter Mons).*

Stoke Park
Approach via Stoke Bruerne or by footpath from lock 20. ½m west of the canal. Built 1629-35 by Inigo Jones. The exterior and gardens of Stoke Park House (now demolished), may be visited. *Open July-Aug, Sat & Sun only.*

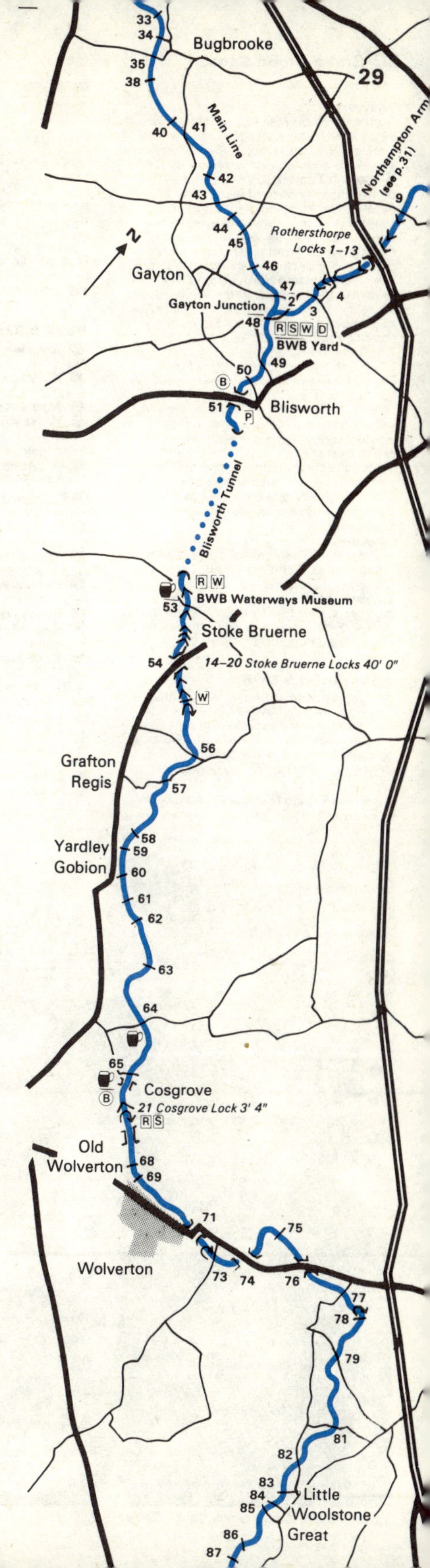

Blisworth
Northants. Pop 1190. PO, tel. stores, garage. Large brown stone village. The church, just E of the canal, is mostly 14thC. Blisworth stone was quarried extensively in the 18thC.
Blisworth Tunnel 3057 yards long. Blisworth is the second longest navigable canal tunnel in Britain. No towpath, but the channel is wide enough to allow the passing of two 7ft boats; so keep to the right. *Boats over 7ft beam must give advance notice to the section inspector at Gayton (Tel: Northampton 858233) or to the lock keeper or the manager at the Waterways Museum, Stoke Bruerne (Roade 862229) so that boats can be prevented from entering the tunnel at the opposite end.* The Grand Junction Canal was opened in 1800 with the exception of this tunnel. The first attempt at excavation failed, so a tramway was built over Blisworth Hill, linking the two termini. Boats arriving at either end had to be unloaded on to horse-drawn waggons, which were then pulled over the hill, and reloaded on to boats. A second attempt at the tunnel was successful, and it opened on 25th March, 1805. Originally boats were legged through. (Note the leggers' hut at the south end).
Gayton
Northants. PO, tel. stores. Large, handsome stone houses, 16thC to 19thC. Large church with ornamented tower.
Bugbrooke
Northants. Pop 1180. EC Sat. PO, tel. stores, garage. Fine 18thC houses to the south and a Baptist church of 1808. Partly 13thC parish church.

BOATYARDS & BWB

(B) **Cosgrove Marina** The Lock House, Cosgrove (Milton Keynes 562467). D Gas, mooring, crane, slipway nearby. A mobile breakdown service is also available.

(B) **BWB Gayton Yard** Blisworth. (858233). R S W D Moorings, slipway, toilets.

(B) **Black Prince Narrow Boats** Gayton rd, Blisworth (858868). R S W P Pump-out (*not winter weekends*). Boat hire, gas, repairs, mooring, toilets.

CRUISES

Linda Cruises Cosgrove Lock. (Milton Keynes 563377). D Boat and engine repairs, toilets, provisions. Full-length narrow boat carries up to 40 passengers on variety of cruises from 2-6 hours. All available only to private parties. (On bank holidays, trips for public from Stoke Bruerne.) Food on board can be arranged. Enquiries to Linda Cruises, Cosgrove Lock, Milton Keynes, Bucks.

PUBS & RESTAURANTS

New Inn New Bradwell, near bridge 73. Food.
Black Horse Black Horse Bridge, Great Linford. Canalside. Food.
Nag's Head Great Linford.
Navigation Inn Castlethorpe Wharf, Cosgrove. (Yardley Gobion 205). Canalside. Food, garden.
Barley Mow Cosgrove. Canalside. Skittles. Snacks, meals, gardens, mooring.
Cosgrove Lodge Hotel Cosgrove. (Stony Stratford 2180). Restaurant.
Galleon Inn Old Wolverton. (376). Canalside, at bridge 68. Food.
White Hart Grafton Regis. (Yardley Gobion 676). On A508 west of canal. Food.
Coffee Pot Yardley Gobion. (206). Food.
Royal Oak Blisworth. Food, garden.
Sun, Moon & Stars Cafe High st, Blisworth. (234). Food.
Boat Inn Stoke Bruerne. (Roade 862428). Canalside. Food, skittles.
Butty Stoke Bruerne. Italian Food. Reservation advisable, ring Roade 863654.
Bakers Arms High st, Bugbrooke. Garden.
Five Bells 14 Church lane, Bugbrooke. Garden.
Eyken Arms Gayton.
Queen Victoria Inn Gayton. (Blisworth 438). Restaurant.

Stoke Bruerne, Grand Union Canal. *Derek Pratt.*

Northampton

5 miles

The Northampton arm falls away steeply from Gayton Junction, towards Northampton where it connects with the navigable River Nene (to Peterborough, the Fens and the Wash). The main feature of the arm is the flight of 17 locks down to Northampton. The traditional drawbridges that cross the canal look pretty but are hard work to operate. The entry into Northampton passes factories, disused warehouses and railway junctions. Anyone considering stopping in the town is advised to pass through the bottom lock and into the Nene navigation where the surroundings are more inviting.

Navigational note
The river Nene is a fully navigable river from Northampton down to the Wash. At Peterborough, which is 60 miles and 37 locks away, the river becomes tidal. Boats using the river need ordinary Grand Union-sized $1\frac{1}{4}$" windlasses, and also a set of special lock keys. These must be obtained from the Northampton Toll Collector's office, which is by South bridge, Northampton (38019). Information and permission to navigate the river should in any case be sought from the Welland & Nene River Authority, North st, Oundle, Peterborough (Oundle 3366).

Rothersthorpe
Northants. Pop 240. EC Sat. PO, tel, stores. The church contains a Tudor pulpit. W of the village is a circular dovecot with 900 nesting places.

Milton Malsor
Northants. Pop 680. PO, tel, stores. 14thC church. Several elegant stone houses of the 17thC and 18thC.

Northampton
Northants. Pop 121,890. EC Thur. MD Wed/Sat. All services. Largely destroyed by fire in 1675. Now a rapidly expanding centre of the shoe industry. Only the archway remains of the 12thC Norman castle where Thomas à Beckett was tried in 1164. There are several churches of interest, including a rare round Norman one of c.1110.

Abingdon Museum Abingdon Park. Period rooms, toys, bygones, Northampton lace, ceramics, natural history. *Closed Sun in winter.*

Central Museum and Art Gallery Guildhall rd. Archaeology, antiquities, paintings, furniture and one of the finest collection of historical footwear in Europe, including Queen Victoria's wedding shoes, and ballet shoes worn by Nijinsky.

Delapre Abbey London rd (A50), $\frac{1}{2}$ mile south of canal. A former Cluniac nunnery, founded in 1145, the Abbey underwent major alterations in the 16thC and 17thC. *Open Thur & Sat afternoon.* S of the Abbey park is Eleanor Cross, one of three surviving crosses set up by Edward I in 1290 to mark the last resting places of Queen Eleanor on her way to burial in Westminster Abbey.

Battle of Northampton 10th July, 1460 ½m S of Northampton Lock, between Delapre Abbey and Hunsbury Hill. A significant battle in the Wars of the Roses in which the Lancastrian King Henry was defeated by Edward of York.

PUBS & RESTAURANTS

- **Chequers** Rothersthorpe. Food.
- **Greyhound** Milton Malsor. Food.
- ✕ **Plough Hotel** Bridge st, Northampton. (38401). Food (except weekends), accommodation.

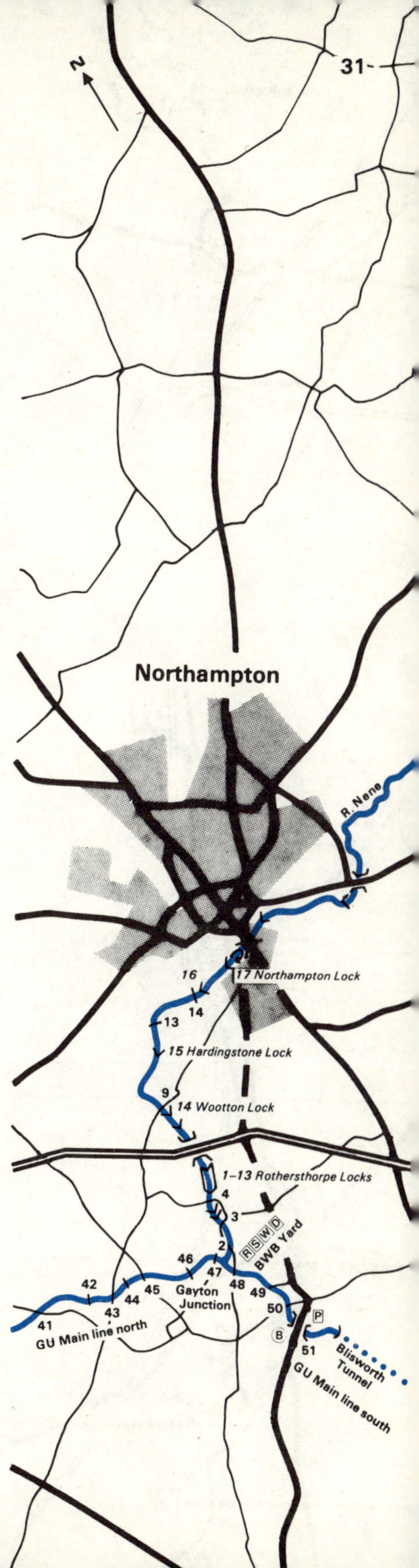

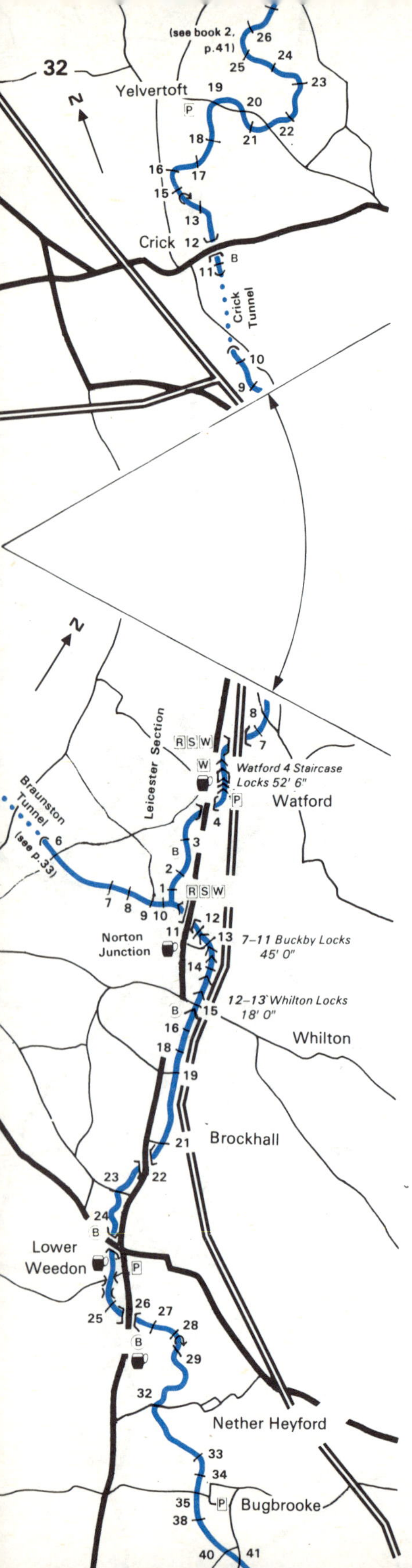

Watford

Gayton Junction to Norton Junction 12 miles

The canal begins to meander sharply towards Norton Junction where the main line turns west and the attractive Leicester Section continues northwards.

Nether Heyford
Northants. Pop 730. PO, tel, stores.
Weedon
Northants. Pop 1490. EC Thur. PO, tel, stores, garage. The Victorian church has a Norman tower. To the north are the remains of Weedon barracks.
Brockhall
Northants. PO box. Tudor Hall with fine 18thC interiors.
Whilton
Northants. PO, tel, stores. 1m E of canal. The site of Banaventa, a Roman settlement, lies to the west.
Buckby Wharf
Northants. PO box, tel, stores.
Watford
Northants. Pop 230. EC Sat. PO, tel, stores. The 13thC church contains some interesting monuments. Watford Court is partly 17thC with Victorian additions.
Crick
Northants. Pop 780. PO, tel, stores. The large church contains much decorative stonework and a circular font.
Crick Tunnel 1528 yards long. Opened in 1814. Quicksands caused a change of route, greatly affecting work.
Yelvertoft
Northants. Pop 450. PO, tel, stores, garage.
Winwick
Northants. 1m SE bridge 23. A semi-deserted village. Surviving 16thC Manor House with Tudor gateway.

BOATYARDS & BWB

Ⓑ **Concoform Marine** The Boatyard, High st, Weedon. (40739). W P D Pump-out, moorings, slipway, gas, hire narrow boats. *Open Tues-Sat summer, Mon-Fri winter.*
Ⓑ **Waterways Holidays** Stowe Hill Wharf, Weedon. (41365) R S W D Pump-out, repairs, gas, narrow boat and day boat hire. Dry dock, boat building and repairs, mooring, toilets, provisions. *Closed Sun.*
Ⓑ **Whilton Marine** Whilton locks. (Long Buckby (842577). R S W P D Moorings, repairs, chandlery, groceries, hire cruisers, slipway, clubhouse, toilets, showers. Bar.
Ⓑ **Weltonfield Narrowboats** Weltonfield Farm, bridge 2. (Long Buckby 842282) R S W D Pump-out (telephone in advance). Boat hire, gas, boat building and repairs, toilets, shop, boat lift.

PUBS & RESTAURANTS

New Inn Weedon, near bridge 24.
✕ **Crossroads Hotel** Weedon. (354). Food.
Narrow Boat Weedon. (336). Canalside, at bridge 26. Sandwiches and snacks.
Stag's Head Watford Gap. Canalside.
New Inn Canalside, at Buckby Top lock.
White Horse Norton (1½m W of bridge 15).
✕ **Red Lion Inn** Main st, Crick. (342). Food, skittles.
Wheatsheaf 15 Main st, Crick. (284).
Knightly Arms High st, Yelvertoft. Food.

Braunston

18 miles

From Norton Junction the canal runs westwards towards Braunston, a big canal centre. A large boatyard situated on an arm to the south meets every boating need. The arm was part of the old route to Oxford before it was shortened by building a large embankment (Braunston Puddle Bank) across the Leam valley to Braunston Turn. Leaving Braunston, the Grand Union joins the Oxford Canal to Napton Junction, a pleasant lock-free stretch. At Calcutt Locks the descent towards Warwick begins, passing the Stockton industrial belt.

Welton
Northants. PO, tel, stores.

Braunston
Northants. Pop 1190. PO, tel, stores, launderette. The village is a well known canal centre. A fine selection of old buildings line the canal. The shop, by the bottom lock, is full of all sorts of canal relics and ephemera.

Braunston Tunnel 2042 yards long, opened in 1796, its construction was hindered by quicksands. *Two boats of 7ft beam can pass in this tunnel, but wide beam boats must get permission from the lock-keepers at Buckby (Long Buckby 234) or Braunston (Rugby 890259) to enter the tunnel. They will then give a clear passage.*

Lower Shuckburgh
Northants. Pop 70. Post box. The church, built 1846, contains much contrasting brickwork.

Stockton
Warwicks. EC Sat. PO, tel, stores, garage. The church is built of Blue Lias, quarried near Stockton Locks.

Long Itchington
Warwicks. Pop 1680. PO, tel, stores, garage. Attractive village with 17thC and 18thC houses and a largely 13thC church.

BOATYARDS & BWB

Ⓑ **Ladyline/Braunstone Marina** Braunston. (Rugby 890325). R S W P D Moorings, repairs, chandlery, dry dock, slipway, hire, food, toilets, showers, gas.

Ⓑ **Calcutt Boats** Calcutt Top Lock, Stockton, Rugby. (Southam 3757). S W D Pump-out. Boat hire, slipway, gas, dry dock, boat building and repairs, mooring, chandlery, toilets, provisions. Charter and hotel boats.

PUBS & RESTAURANTS

Admiral Nelson Little Braunston. Canalside, at lock 3. 'Canals' decor of prints and lace plates. Food, skittles.

White Horse Welton. Food, skittles.

New Inn Buckby Top Lock. Canalside.

✕ **The Boatman** Braunston. (Rugby 890313). Popular canalside pub at Braunston Turn. Bar snacks; garden with swings. Meals every day except Sun evening and all day Mon.

The Old Plough Braunston. Food.

Two Boats Inn Long Itchington. Br 25.

Blue Lias Stockton. (Southam 2249). Canalside, at bridge 23. Food, fine selection of malt whiskies. Animals in garden.

Boat Birdingbury wharf. Canalside, at bridge 21. Food.

✕ **Cuttle Inn** Long Itchington. Canalside. Petrol adjacent.

Two Boats Inn Long Itchington. Canalside. Food.

Plenty of pubs in Long Itchington village.

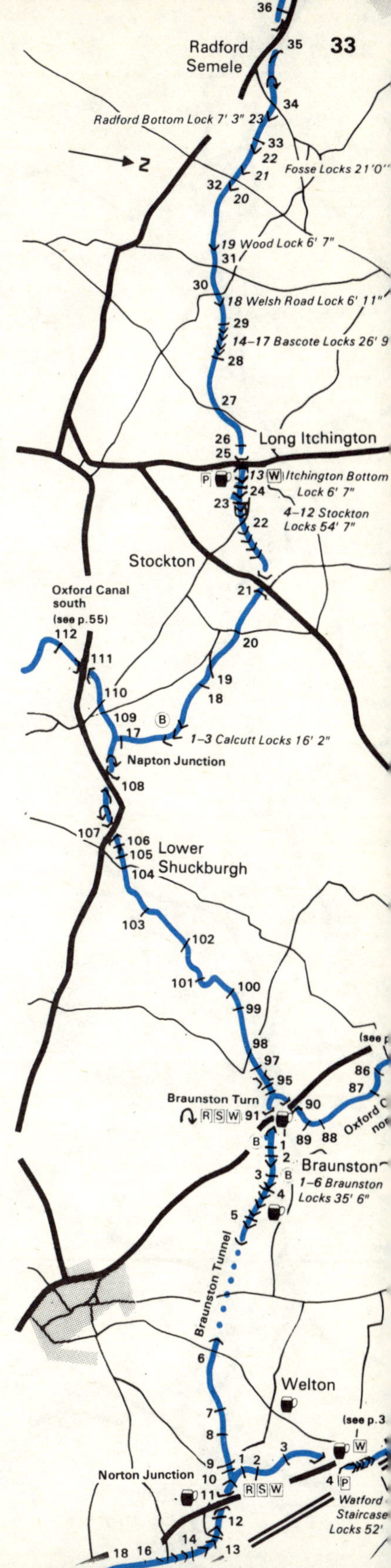

Royal Leamington Spa

16 miles

From Fosse Locks the canal continues west, straight through Leamington, then swings north west towards Warwick which is best approached from bridge 46. As the canal skirts round the town to Budbrooke Junction, where the old Warwick and Napton Canal joined the Warwick and Birmingham, the arm leading into Warwick is now disused. West of Budbrooke Junction is the first of the 21 daunting Hatton Locks. At Kingswood is the junction with the Stratford-upon-Avon Canal, restored by volunteers in 1964, and now owned by the National Trust. The Stratford-on-Avon Canal Manager's office at Kingswood Junction (Lapworth 3370) will give information on the canal. After Kingswood, the canal moves north towards Solihull across the midland watershed. The remains of the old locks at Knowle can be seen alongside the new, together with the sidepond. These are the northernmost wide locks for many miles.

Radford Semele
Warwicks. Pop 1270. EC Thur. PO, tel, stores, garage. Suburb of Leamington. Radford Hall is a reconstructed Jacobean building. The church is Victorian.

Offchurch
Warwicks. PO, tel, stores, garage. Residential village. The church with its tall grey stone tower contains some Norman work. To the west lies Offchurch Bury, originally a 17thC house, now with a Gothic façade.

Royal Leamington Spa
Warwicks. Pop 44,970. EC Mon/Thur. All services. A largely mid-Victorian spa town. J. Cundall, a local architect of some note designed several buildings including the town hall. Since the Victorian era much industrialisation has taken place.

Art Gallery & Museum Avenue rd. British, Dutch and Flemish paintings of the 16thC and 17thC. Also modern art, pottery, porcelain and 18thC English drinking glasses. Victorian costume and objects. *Open daily.*

All Saints' Church Bath st. Begun in 1843 to the design of J. C. Jackson, the church is of Gothic style, not always correct in detail. The north transept has a rose window patterned on Rouen Cathedral; the west window is by Kempe.

Jephson Gardens Alongside Newbold terrace, north of bridge 40. Beautiful ornamental gardens named after Dr Jephson (1798-1878), the local practitioner who was largely responsible for the spa's high medical reputation.

Information Bureau Royal Pump Room, Dormer place. (21215).

Warwick
Warwicks. Pop 18,690. EC Thur. MD Wed/Sat. All services. Historic town which still contains many medieval buildings.

Church of St Mary's Of Norman origin, it contains a large 12thC crypt. Much of the building was burnt down in 1694. The rebuilt church has a pseudo-Gothic tower.

Warwick County Museum Market place. Mainly local interest. Includes the Sheldon tapestry map of Warwickshire which dates from 1588. *Open daily, closed Fri; Sun winter.*

Doll Museum Oken's House, Castle st. *Open daily.*

Court House Jury st. The present building which dates from 1725, was built on the site of a 16thC civic building.

Lord Leycester Hospital High st. The hospital was founded by the Earl of Leycester in 1571. It is now a hospital for retired or disabled Servicemen.

Warwick Castle Castle Hill. The exterior is a famous example of a 14thC fortification. Inside are pictures by Rubens, Van Dyck and Velasquez. Capability Brown grounds. *Open Good Fri-mid Sept daily.*

Hatton
Warwicks. Scattered around the top of the Hatton locks. The church is partly perpendicular, partly Victorian. North of Hatton is Hasely. Its small church still retains box pews and dates from the 13thC.
Shrewley
Warwicks. PO, tel, stores, garage. Useful source of supplies.
Shrewley Tunnel 433 yards long, opened in 1799 with the completion of the Warwick and Birmingham Canal. It is remarkable for the very clearly defined path over the top of the tunnel which a towing horse would use while its boat was 'legged' through the tunnel. This horsepath in fact goes through its own miniature tunnel for 40 yards and emerges at the north west end above and beside the canal tunnel.
This tunnel allows two 7ft boats to pass; keep to the right.
Rowington
Warwicks. Pop 790. PO, tel, stores. Some 17thC and 18thC buildings. The 13thC church by the canal has a fine peal of bells.
Wroxall
Warwicks. 1½m NE of Rowington. Remains of Benedictine Abbey founded in c.1135. Its church with a 14thC nave and 17thC tower survives. A gloomy Victorian mansion replaced a Tudor house bought by Sir Christopher Wren for his son in 1713.
Kingswood
Warwicks. All services. The village is scattered over a wide area from the Grand Union to the Stratford-on-Avon Canal. The centre is 1m to the west, around the ambitious 15thC church. The main feature of interest is the canal junction. Note particularly the iron turnover bridge by the lock at the junction which is split to allow the towing rope to pass through without being unhitched from the horse. Such bridges are a feature of the Stratford-on-Avon Canal.
Packwood House
Hockley Heath. 2m W of bridge 66. (Lapworth 2024). Timber-framed Tudor house, enlarged in the 17thC. Tapestry, needlework and furniture. The 17thC yew garden was laid out to represent the Sermon on the Mount, the trees taking the place of Jesus and his followers. *Open afternoons. Apr-Sept, closed Mon, Fri. Oct-Mar, open Wed, Sat, Sun, Bank Hols.* National Trust property.

BOATYARDS & BWB
Ⓑ **BWB Hatton Workshops** Canal la, Hatton, Warwick – near the top Hatton Locks. (42192). [S] [W] Dry dock available for hire, also crane for boats up to 2 tons.
Ⓑ **Boats (Warwick)** Nelson lane, Warwick. (42968). [S] [W] [D] Pump-out. Boat hire, gas, chandlery, toilets. *Closed Sun.*

PUBS & RESTAURANTS
Moore's Cafe 41 The Parade, Leamington Spa. Food. *Closed Sun.*
Il Portico 50 Clarendon st, Leamington Spa. (24471). Italian food. *Closed Sun.*
Stag Inn Offchurch. Food.
White Lion Inn Radford Semele. (Leamington Spa 25770/20230). Food *(except Sun)*. Coaching inn, built in 1622. Garden.
Aylesford Restaurant 1 High st, Warwick. (42799). Extensive menu. *(Closed Sun.)*
New Inn Hatton. (Warwick 42427). Lunches & dinners *(except Sun)*.
Cape of Good Hope Cape Locks, Warwick. Canalside. Food.
Lord Leycester Hotel Jury st, Warwick. (41481). Restaurant.
Westgate Arms Bowling Green st, Warwick. (42362).
Navigation Kingswood. Canalside. Food.
Ye Olde New Inn Turners green, Rowington. Canalside. Food.
Cockhorse Inn Rowington. Food.
Durham Ox Shrewley. Food.
Chadwick Manor Hotel Knowle. (2821). Food, residential.
Coffee Pot 2 Station rd, Knowle. (5554). Food. *EC Thur. Closed Sun.*
Black Boy Knowle, Canalside, at bridge 69. Food.
Florentine 15 Kenilworth rd, Knowle. (6449). Italian cooking. *Closed Sun; Mon L; B. Hols.*

Grand Union main line

Birmingham

5 miles

Continuing north west, the canal passes through Birmingham's expanding suburbia. Supplies are available in plenty, but the embankment makes access rather difficult. Beyond Olton Bridge, housing estates and disused wharves accompany the canal, and boatmen should be wary of rubbish in the water. Access to and from the canal becomes increasingly difficult. Camp Hill Locks and all the succeeding locks are narrow – only boats of 7ft beam or less can pass. The former Birmingham and Warwick Junction Canal runs north from Bordesley Junction to join the Birmingham and Fazeley and Tame Valley Canals at Salford Junction. It was opened in 1844 to by-pass the heavily locked stretches of the B & F at Ashted and Aston. The five Garrison Locks carry the canal down to the Erdington level where there is a stop lock.
Birmingham and its canal navigations are described in full in the 'Guide to the Waterways – Midlands', book 2 in the series.

Catherine de Barnes
West Midlands. Tel, stores, garage. A convenient supply centre with easy access from the canal.
Solihull
West Midlands. Pop 110,000. EC Wed. All services. A modern commuter development, with fine public buildings. The church is almost all 14thC. The interior contains work of all periods, 17thC pulpit and communion rail, 19thC stained glass.
Elmdon Heath
West Midlands. EC Thur. PO, tel, stores, garage. Suburb of Solihull. Source of supplies for the athletic. Climb up the embankment by bridge 79.
Tyseley Goods Yard ¼m SW of bridge 88. Here the Standard Gauge Steam Trust has a large depot for maintaining, storing and running private steam railway engines. *Open to visitors weekends April to October* (there is usually at least one locomotive in steam every Sunday) and on 2 big open days every summer. For details write to the Trust at 24 Harborne rd, Edgbaston, Birmingham 15.
Birmingham
West Midlands. Pop 1,107,200. EC Wed. MD Thur. All services. The Bull Ring, one of the most modern shopping centres in Europe, used to be the village green. Now an industrial and commercial city, Birmingham is famous for such men as John Baskerville, William Murdoch, Joseph Priestly, Matthew Boulton and James Watt.
Assay Office Newhall st. (236 6951). Silverware, coins, tokens and medals. Also the Matthew Boulton collection of correspondence and books. *Open by appointment only.*
Aston Hall Frederick rd. 2m N of city. A Jacobean house built by Sir Thomas Holte in 1618-35. Many of the rooms are furnished in period, and there are impressive friezes and ceilings. *Open daily.*
Avery Historical Museum Soho Foundry (558 1112). Machines, instruments, weights and records illustrating the history of weighing. *By appointment only.*

Birmingham (cont)

Barber Institute of Fine Arts The University, Edgbaston. Masterpieces by Bellini, Degas, Courbet, Rubens, Rembrandt, Reynolds Gainsborough and other artists before 1900. *Open Mon-Fri, 1st Sun afternoon of every month during term-time.*

Birmingham City Museum & Art Gallery Congreve st. One of the most important museums outside London, with departments of art, ethnography, archaeology, natural history, science and industry. Fine Old Master paintings and an exceptional collection of Pre-Raphaelites. Famous Pinto collections of by-gones and an unusual number of industrial relics. *For opening times ring Information Bureau (235 3411).*

Cannon Hill Museum Pershore rd. Designed primarily for children. Illustrated leisure time pursuits including bird-watching, bee-keeping, fishing and pets; Safari hut around which the sounds, sights—and smells of the African Bush are recreated.

Geological Departmental Museum The University, Edgbaston. Includes the Holcroft collection of fossils and the Lapworth collection of grapholites. *Open daily by arrangement.*

Sarehole Mill Colebank rd, Hall Green. An 18thC water powered corn mill, once used by Matthew Boulton for metal working and blade grinding. It is still in working order. *Open daily 14.00-19.00 (Sat 11.00-19.00).*

Farmers Bridge An exciting canalside development at Cambrian wharf (the end of the Birmingham & Fazeley Canal, not shown on the map) in which four sky-scrapers, a new canal pub and a restored 18thC street complete with gaslights are grouped beside a recently restored canal basin. The pub is totally canal orientated, sporting much canal paraphernalia and a bar in genuine floating narrow boat. One of the 18thC houses is a canal shop and information centre. Good mooring.

Cannon Hill Edgbaston. Formal gardens, including a Japanese Garden of Contemplation, tropical and sub-tropical plants, adjacent.

Edgbaston Reservoir A 60-acre lake which feeds the Birmingham Canal; sailing and rowing facilities.

Lickey Hills SW boundary of city. 500 acres of hill and moorland. Pony trekking.

Olton Reservoir Near Olton Station. Feeds the Grand Union Canal and floats a medley of sailing boats.

Information Bureau The Council House, Victoria square, Birmingham 1. (235 3411). Weekly information leaflet available from here and from banks and libraries.

BOATYARDS & BWB

Canal shop & Information Centre 2 Kingston row, Birmingham 1. (236 4844). R S W Moorings, chandlery, toilets, provisions. *Closed Sun.*

PUBS & RESTAURANTS

Boat Inn Catherine de Barnes. Food.

Long Boat Farmers bridge top lock, Kingston row, Birmingham 1. Canalside. Food.

Gino's Bull Ring Centre. (643 2966). Restaurant.

Sandonia Restaurant 509 Hagley rd, Bimringham 17. (429 2622). Restaurant (Cypriot).

La Capanna Hurst st, Birmingham. (021-622 2287). Italian restaurant. *Closed Sun.*

Danish Food Centre 10 Stephenson Place, Birmingham. (021-643 2837). Meals available all day from breakfast to after-theatre supper. *Closed Sun; Mon D.*

Salamis Kebab House 178 Broad st, Edgbaston, Birmingham. (021-643 2997). Friendly Greek restaurant. Dinner only (18.00-24.00). *Closed L; B. Hols.*

Kennet & Avon Canal

The Kennet & Avon Canal was built in three stages. The first two were river navigations, the Kennet from Reading to Newbury (built 1718-23), and the Avon from Bath to Bristol (built 1725-27). Both were engineered by John Hore. The third stage, a canal from Newbury to Bath was authorised in 1794 and opened in 1810. Rennie was the engineer/architect. His architecture was exceptional, but there were grave defects in his engineering. A short summit level necessitated a steam pumping station at Crofton; and a water powered one at Claverton had to make up for the constant leakage through the porous rock of the canal bed.

The canal has many remarkable features. The 29 lock flight at Devizes is the most spectacular in England, and the canal's elegant architecture contributes to the landscape. The swing bridges run on ball bearings, one of the first applications of the principle.

The Kennet & Avon Canal took over the two river navigations, thus forming the major east-west canal route. However traffic was never heavy and the canal declined in the 19thC. Today, although through navigation is impossible, the K & A Trust and the BWB seem likely to re-open the canal during the 80's.

Maximum dimensions

Reading to Bath, junction with river Avon

Length: 71′ or 67′

Beam: at 7′ or at 13′ 9″

Headroom: 7′ 6″

Bath to Hanham lock

Length: 75′, Beam: 16′, Headroom: 8′ 9″

Mileage

READING to

Tile Mill lock: 8

Aldermaston Wharf: 10

Newbury lock: 18½

Kintbury: 24½

Hungerford: 27½

Crofton top lock: 35

Pewsey Wharf: 41½

Devizes top lock: 53½

Bradford-on-Avon: 65½

Dundas Aqueduct: 70

Bath, junction with river Avon: 75¼

HANHAM lock (start of tidal section): 86½

Total 107 locks

---

9 miles

The Kennet leaves the Thames and runs south west towards the centre of Reading, passing Blake's Lock which is maintained by the Thames Water Authority. The Kennet through Reading is narrow, shallow and fast flowing. Several blind bends in the town call for careful navigation. Remember to look out for other boats and allow for the flow of the river. Weirs should be treated with respect as the current they create can often affect the course of a boat, especially when making a slow approach to a lock. At Theale is the first of the swing bridges that occur along the Kennet & Avon. Opening the bridge is hard work, but there are intructions to help you. Make sure you close the traffic barriers first and leave them open behind you.

Navigational note. Whilst in theory a vessel of 13′ 9″ beam will be able to traverse the canal when it is restored, in practice two vessels of this width would have difficulty in passing in many places. So in practice the maximum beam is in the order of 7ft.

Reading
Berks. Pop 124,000. EC Mon/Wed. MD Mon. All services. The town is interesting for its Victorian architecture. There is no towing path by the canal in the town centre; however west of Reading the whole canal is a public right of way.
Abbey Ruins Remains of the 12thC abbey built by Henry I lie on the edge of Forbury Park. 13thC gatehouse, altered 1869.
The Gaol Forbury rd. Designed by Scott and Moffat in 1842-4 in the Scottish baronial style.
St Bartholomew London rd. Built mainly by Waterhouse, 1879; chancel by Bodley, 1881. Decorations by Sir Ninian Comper.
Museum of English Rural Life White-knights Park. Reading 85123, ext. 475. Includes agricultural relics and a small display of canal interest. *Open Tue-Sat. Closed Sun, Mon, B. Hols.*

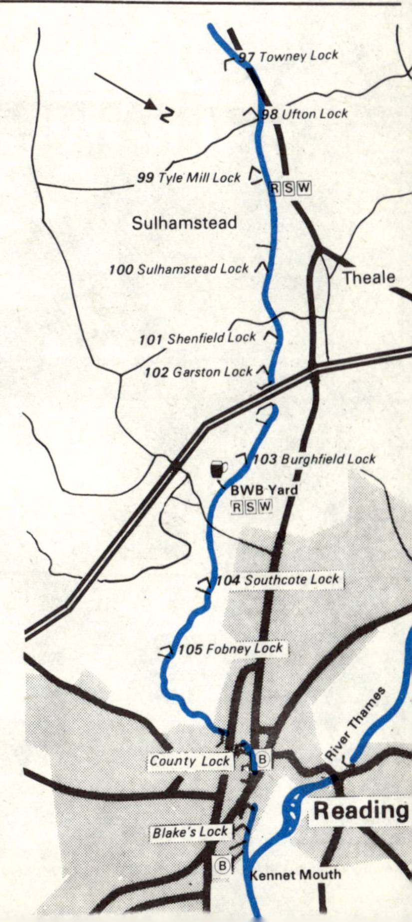

Museum & Art Gallery Friar st. Includes natural history, local archaeology and prehistoric collections. *Open weekdays.*

Theale
Berks. Pop 1638. EC Wed. All services. The Gothic revival church, built by Garbett (1820-32), is essentially a miniature version of Salisbury Cathedral.

Sulhamstead
Berks. PO, tel, stores. See Folly Farm for a successful integration of William and Mary and vernacular Tudor styles.

BOATYARDS & BWB

Ⓑ **Kennet Mouth Boatyard** Kennetside, Reading. (64186). [W][D] Pump-out. Boat hire, slip way, gas, boat building and repairs, overnight mooring, provisions. *Open summer only.*

Ⓑ **Reading Marine Co.** Crane wharf, Kings rd, Reading. (53917) [R][W][D] Pump-out. Boat hire, slipway, gas, boat and engine repairs, mooring, chandlery, toilets. *Open summer only.*

Ⓑ **BWB** Burghfield bridge. Enquiries to BWB Section Inspector, Lower wharf, Padworth, Reading. (Woolhampton 2277) [R][S][W] Moorings. BWB car park.

CRUISES

Kennet Cruises (K & A Canal Trust), 14 Beach lane, Earley, Reading. (81115). Public trips from Reading to Tyle Mill. *Weekends & B. Hols.* Private charter – up to 49 passengers.

PUBS & RESTAURANTS

Cooper's Wine Lodge 29 Market place, Reading. (52238). Food *(lunch only except Sat).*

Chez Viktor 66 George st, Reading (476761). Bistro. Relaxed and friendly. *Closed Sun; L; B. Hols.* Must book.

Mama Mia 11 St Mary's Butts, Reading. (581357). Cheerful trattoria. *Closed Sun; B. Hols.*

Jolly Anglers Kennetside, Reading. Canalside. Food, water.

Thames Tavern Kennetside, Reading. Canalside. Food.

Three Kings Jacks Booth Bath rd, Sulhamstead. ½m N of Tyle Mill.

Cunning Man Burghfield bridge. Canalside. Food (hot lunches).

Knight's Farm Restaurant Burghfield. (Reading 52366). ½m S of Burghfield Bridge. International cooking. *Closed Mon; Sun D.*

THE KENNET & AVON CANAL TRUST

Treasurer: 21 Hewett Avenue, Caversham, Reading, Berks. Having re-opened over three-quarters of the canal to navigation, the Trust is now engaged in restoring, among other things, the massive Caen Hill flight of locks. What seemed a pipe dream 10 years ago – navigation from the Thames to the Severn – now seems certain during the 1980's.

Newbury bridge and lock, Kennet and Avon. *Hugh McKnight.*

Newbury

18 miles (not all navigable)

Navigation is now possible to above the recently restored Towney Lock. (An average length boat should be able to turn above this point.) Beyond Ham Mills Lock, the Kennet & Avon is fully navigable for 13½ miles, forming the Newbury Cruiseway which now extends to Potter's Lock.

Aldermaston
Berks. PO, stores.

Aldermaston Wharf
Berks. PO, tel, stores, station. Canalside settlement. Derelict lock, sealed up swing bridge, thriving pub.

Woolhampton
Berks. Pop 840. PO, tel, stores, station. See Midgham station, Woolhampton park and Douai abbey and school.

Thatcham
Pop 1480. EC Wed. PO, tel, stores, station. 14thC chapel–now a school.

Newbury
Berks. Pop 22,170. EC Wed. MD Tue. All services. Light industry. Good shopping. Newbury Fair. *Thur following 11 Oct.* Newbury lock is unusual in having lever operated ground paddles.

St Nicholas Church West Mills. Large perpendicular church, c.1500, with unusual 17thC pulpit.

Borough Museum Wharf rd. Local history, natural history. *Closed Sun, EC Wed.*

Kintbury
Berks. PO, tel, stores, station. The 13thC church was restored in 1859. The Mill is now a restaurant.

BOATYARDS & BWB

BWB Burghfield Bridge Lower wharf. (Woolhampton 2277). R S W Information. Windlasses K & A-sized sold. Enquiries to Section Inspector, Padworth Yard, Lower Wharf, Padworth.

Ⓑ. **Newbury Boat Co** Greenham. (Newbury 30306) R S W D Slipway, gas, boat and engine repairs, mooring. Working boats for hire. *Mon-Fri.*

BOAT TRIPS

Kennet Horse Boat Co 32 Gloucester rd, Newbury, Berks. (44154). Horse-drawn and motor barge. Mostly private charter. *Easter-end Sept.* Public trips on the motor barge *Sun, B. Hols, some weekdays Aug.* Must book.

PUBS & RESTAURANTS

Coach & Horses on A4 E of Oxlease swivel bridge. Food.

Row Barge Woolhampton. (2213). Canalside. Lunches daily. Dinner, *closed Sun, Mon & Tue.*

Angel Hotel Woolhampton. (3307). Food.

Butts Inn Aldermaston wharf. Food.

Hinds Head Aldermaston. Food.

Hare & Hounds on A4 E of Padworth swing bridge.

Out of Town near Hare & Hounds.

Swan Hotel near Thatcham station.

Vane's 7 High st, Thatcham. (63344). Named after Charles Dundas, chairman of the K & A Canal Co. French menu. *L Sun only; D Tue-Sat.*

Coach and Horses ½m N of Midgham bridge. Food.

La Rivièra 26 The Broadway, Newbury. (42074). Greek restaurant. Must book. *Closed Wed & B. Hols.*

Tudor Cafe by Swan bridge, Newbury.

White House by Swan bridge, Newbury. Food.

Old Mill Kintbury. (517/8). Close to Kintbury lock.

Dundas Arms Kintbury. (263). Named after Charles Dundas, chairman of the K & A Canal Co. French menu. *L Sun only; D Tue-Sat.*

White Hart Hamstead Marshall. (Kintbury 201). Good food.

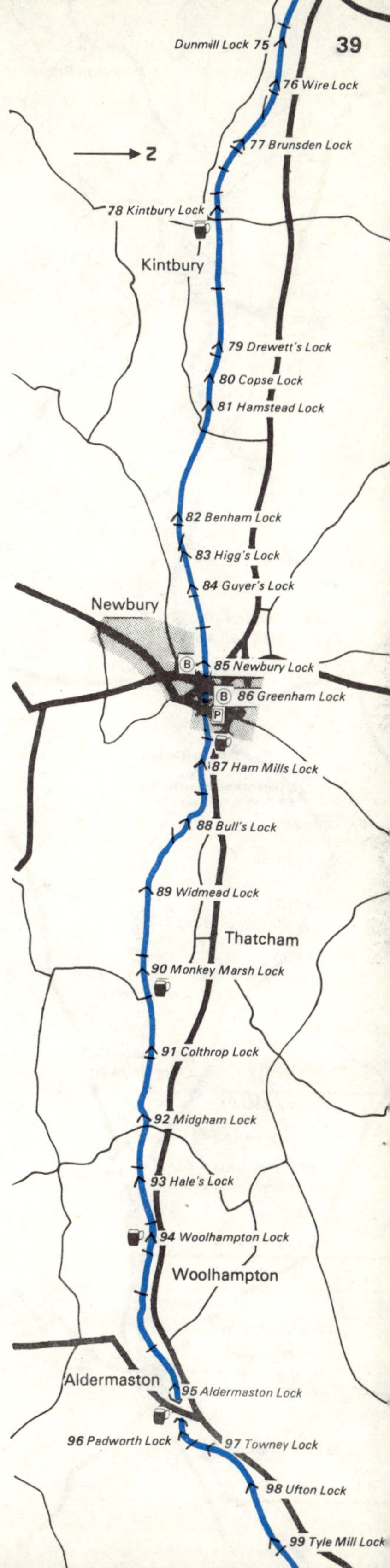

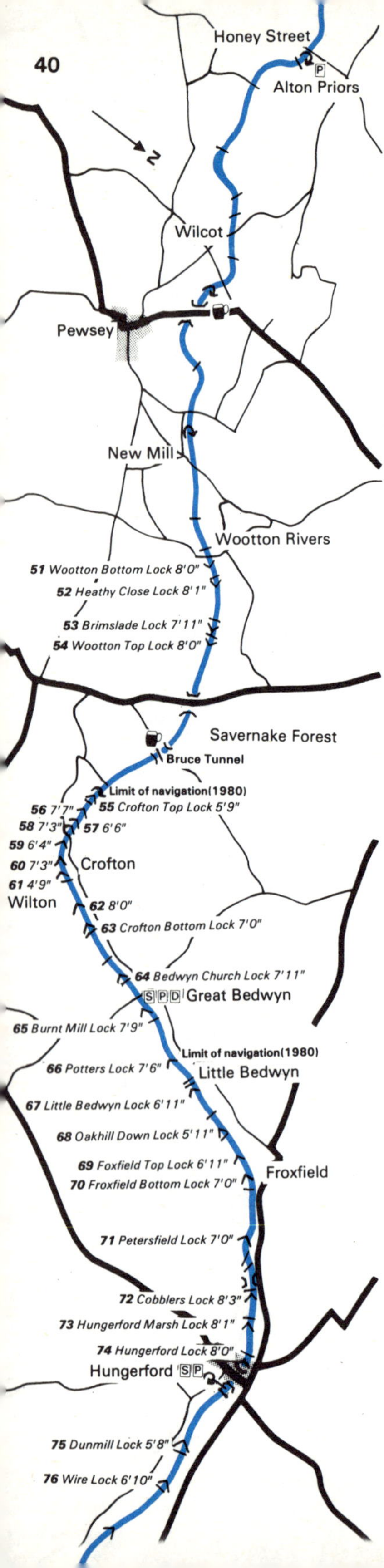

Honey Street
Alton Priors
Wilcot
Pewsey
New Mill
Wootton Rivers
51 Wootton Bottom Lock 8'0"
52 Heathy Close Lock 8'1"
53 Brimslade Lock 7'11"
54 Wootton Top Lock 8'0"
Savernake Forest
Bruce Tunnel
Limit of navigation(1980)
55 Crofton Top Lock 5'9"
56 7'7"
57 6'6"
58 7'3"
59 6'4"
60 7'3"
Crofton
61 4'9"
Wilton
62 8'0"
63 Crofton Bottom Lock 7'0"
64 Bedwyn Church Lock 7'11"
Great Bedwyn
65 Burnt Mill Lock 7'9"
Limit of navigation(1980)
66 Potters Lock 7'6"
Little Bedwyn
67 Little Bedwyn Lock 6'11"
68 Oakhill Down Lock 5'11"
69 Foxfield Top Lock 6'11"
Froxfield
70 Froxfield Bottom Lock 7'0"
71 Petersfield Lock 7'0"
72 Cobblers Lock 8'3"
73 Hungerford Marsh Lock 8'1"
74 Hungerford Lock 8'0"
Hungerford
75 Dunmill Lock 5'8"
76 Wire Lock 6'10"

Hungerford

18 miles

The canal continues west through open countryside, passing Hungerford. Potter's Lock marks the present limit of navigation. The canal continues towards its summit. To the south of Crofton lies Wilton Water, a natural lake from which the Crofton pumps draw their supplies. Preliminary restoration work is in progress on parts of the canal west of Crofton and water reappears by lock 57. Navigation is currently possible for 18½ miles from Crofton Top Lock to Devizes Top Lock. Passing Pewsey and Wilcot, the canal enters the Wide Water, an ornamental lake. The far end is spanned by the neo-classical Ladies Bridge, dated 1808.

Hungerford
Berks. Pop 3,700. EC Thur. All services. A pleasant town with a spacious feeling. The manor house was donated by John of Gaunt in 1366; any monarch passing through the town is given a red rose, the Lancastrian emblem, as a token rent. Hungerford Marsh Lock has a swing bridge across the lock chamber, an unusual feature.

Hocktide Ceremonies Held on the *second Tuesday after Easter,* dating from medieval times.

Avington
Berks. The village is best approached along the track that runs east from lock 76. The little church is still wholly Norman.

Little Bedwyn
Wilts. PO, tel. Divided by the canal. The estate village lies to the north, the older farming village to the south.

Froxfield
Wilts. PO, tel, stores. The main feature of the village is the Somerset Hospital, a range of almshouses founded by the Duchess of Somerset in 1694, extended in 1775 and again in 1813.

Bruce Tunnel
Named in honour of Thomas Bruce, Earl of Ailesbury. 502 yds, with chains attached to the walls, to enable boats to be pulled through.

Littlecote
Wilts. 1½ miles N of Froxfield. A Tudor building of the 16thC, Littlecote is the most important brick mansion in Wiltshire. The Great Hall, the armoury and Long Gallery are particularly notable. *Open: Apr-mid Oct. (Sun 14.00–18.00.)* Pre-booked parties of 20 or more will be shown round on any day *by appointment only.* (Hungerford 2509).

Wilton
Wilts. PO, tel, stores. A compact village with a pretty duck pond.

Wiltshire Wildlife Park
½ mile E of Wilton, accessible from the road crossing the tail of lock 61. Family orientated nature reserve, with children's boating pond, pets' corner, picnic sites. No dogs. *Open: Nov-Mar, Sats & Suns only. Mar-Nov daily.*

Crofton
Wilts. The scattered village is dominated by the brick pumping house with its separate chimney. It houses two 19thC steam engines, one built in 1812 by Boulton and Watt, the oldest working beam engine in the world, the other in 1845 by Harveys of Hayle, Cornwall. Both have been restored to working order, and are steamed on several weekends in the year. The pumping house and the engines are open for viewing *every Sunday, 10.00–18.00.* For details of 'steaming' weekends, ring Burbage 810575.

Great Bedwyn
Wilts. PO, tel, stores, garage, station. The large church, with its well-balanced crossing tower is mostly 12thC and 13thC; there are some interesting monuments inside. The road running west to the church passes the amazing Bedwyn Stone Museum.

Bedwyn Stone Museum A varied collection showing the work of seven generations of stone masons. *Open regularly, daylight hours.*

New Mill
Wilts. A pretty hamlet scattered below the canal.

Wootton Rivers
Wilts. PO, tel, stores. Composed almost entirely of timber-framed thatched houses. Even the walls by the canal are thatched. The little church with its wooden bell turret was extensively rebuilt in the 19thC.

Savernake Forest
Wilts. A small village grew up in the 19thC around the hotel and the 2 railway stations, to cater for an early holiday trade. The stations have since vanished, but the hotel thrives on the hill above Bruce Tunnel.

At Burbage Wharf the handsome 148-year-old crane has been restored, using timber from Savernake Forest.

Wilcot
Wilts. PO, tel, stores. There are several thatched houses, a little village school with a prominent bell, and a blacksmith. Parts of the church date from the 12thC, but it was mostly rebuilt in 1876 after a fire. Teas in village shop, also B&B.

Pewsey
Wilts. Pop 2500. EC Wed. All services, though few trains stop at the station.
All the roads radiate from the fine statue of King Alfred, erected in 1911. The church is mostly 13thC and 15thC, but parts of the nave are late Norman: the altar rails were made from timbers of the 'San Josef' captured by Nelson in 1797.

Pewsey White Horse
1½m S of the town. Dating from the 18thC, the horse was re-cut in 1937 to celebrate the coronation of George VI. It is 66ft long.

BOAT TRIPS

The paddle-boat 'Charlotte Dundas' operates trips along the 'long pound' from Honey Street to Pewsey Wharf or Devizes. See page 43.

Jubilee 44 seat boat. Trips from Wootton Rivers to Crofton Top Lock. Mrs Wilson, Winterslow 862155.

PUBS

John of Gaunt Hungerford. (2642). Food. B&B.
Three Swans Hungerford. (2721). Food. B&B.
Thompson's Eating House 17 High st, Hungerford. (2056). Victorian-style restaurant serving French and Swiss food. *Closed Sun, 2 weeks in Mar.*
Harrow Little Bedwyn. In the southern half of the village.
Pelican Froxfield. On A4, ¼ mile N of the new bridge. Food.
Swan Inn Wilton, ½ mile S of lock 61, on road running beside Wilton Water.
Three Tuns Great Bedwyn.
Liddiard Arms New Mill. Bar billiards.
Royal Oak Wootton Rivers. Bar billiards. Very attractive pub in the main street.
Savernake Forest Hotel Savernake Forest. (Burbage 206). Restaurant. The hotel has fishing rights on the canal.
Golden Swan Wilcot. Food, B&B. At the far end of the village, overlooking the green.
French Horn Pewsey. Canalside, on A345 by wharf.
Royal Oak Pewsey. (3426). In town centre.
Phoenix Pewsey. (2458). In town centre. B&B.

Pewsey Wharf, on the 15-mile Pound between Wootton Rivers and Devizes.

Devizes

19 miles

The canal continues westwards. Passing the well preserved Honey Street Wharf it meanders through open countryside, maintaining its level into Devizes. Beyond the disused wharf and the gas works, the long pound ends at the first lock of the famous Caen Hill flight. This major flight starts at lock 44, each wide lock with an enormous side pound. The flight ends at lock 29, but the locks continue to descend, separated by longer pounds. After two swing bridges the canal reaches the first of the five restored Seend Locks, then continues a fairly straight course through a quiet and secluded section. The attractive lock house by lock 15 has been restored. The bridge just beyond the lock is the best access point for Semington. Close examination of the north bank just before the bridge reveals the site of the junction with the old Wiltshire & Berkshire Canal which used to go to Abingdon. The canal is navigable from the bottom of the Caen Hill Flight to Bradford-on-Avon.

Allington
Wilts. Tel. Small agricultural village. All Cannings Cross, a large Iron Age settlement lies to the east.

All Cannings
Wilts. PO, tel, stores. The church, with its tall central tower, is mostly 14thC, although its most interesting feature is the ornamental High Victorian chancel added in 1867.

Stanton St. Bernard
Wilts. PO, tel, stores. The 19thC manor incorporates relics of an earlier house. The battlemented church is Victorian.

Honey Street
Wilts. Traditional canalside village. Brick cottages, a warehouse, a wharf and some weatherboarded buildings.

Alton Barnes
Wilts. PO, tel, stores, garage. Fine farm buildings and an 18thC rectory. The church, essentially Anglo-Saxon, has been heavily restored.

Alton Priors
Wilts. Tel. Approached by footpath from Alton Barnes churchyard; the isolated church is the best feature of this scattered hamlet. The pretty perpendicular building contains a large box tomb surmounted with an engraved Dutch brass plate, dated 1590, rich in extravagant symbolism. To the east of the village, the Ridge Way runs southwards towards Salisbury.

Devizes
Wilts. Pop 9000. EC Wed. MD Thur. PO, tel, stores, garage, bank, station. Retains the atmosphere of an old market town. The market cross records the sad story of Ruth Pierce. The two fine churches, one built for the castle, the other for the parish, tend to dominate. Only the mound and related earthworks survive of the original Norman castle; the present building is an extravagant Victorian folly. The K & A Canal Trust are opening a museum and shop in a converted warehouse by the wharf.

St. John's Church Built by Bishop Roger of Sarum, who was also responsible for the castle. The 12thC church with its massive crossing tower is still largely original with 15thC and 19thC additions.

St. Mary's Church Dates from the same time as St. John's. This church was more extensively rebuilt in the 15thC although much Norman work still remains.

Devizes Museum Long st. Includes the Stourhead collection of relics excavated from the burial mounds on Salisbury Plain. *Open Tues-Sat.*

Battle of Roundway Down, 1643 The site of the Civil War battle lies off the A361 NE of Devizes.

Coate
Wilts. PO, tel. Farming village.

Wiltshire Regiment Museum Le Marchant Barracks, 1½m E of Devizes on A361; also accessible from the canal. The history of the regiment from its foundation in 1756 to the present day. *Open weekdays.*

Devizes to Westminster Canoe Race
The toughest and longest canoe race in the world takes place *every Easter*. The 125 mile course is between Park Road bridge, Devizes, and the County Hall Steps, Westminster.

Bishops Canning
Wilts. PO, tel, stores. The cruciform church with its central tower and spire, is almost entirely early English in style; traces of the earlier Norman building survive.

Seend Cleave
Wilts. Tel, stores. Agricultural village.

Seend
Wilts. PO, tel, stores, garage. 18thC houses; battlemented perpendicular church.

Sells Green
Wilts. PO, tel, garage.

Semington
Wilts. PO, tel, stores, garage. The little stone church, crowned with a bellcote, is at the end of a lane to the east of the village.

The Wiltshire & Berkshire Canal
Opened in 1810, the canal meandered for 51 miles between Semington and Abingdon on the River Thames. A branch was opened in 1819 from Swindon to connect with Latton on the Thames & Severn Canal. Although the carriage of Somerset coal was the inspiration for the canal, its eventual role was agricultural. Profits were never high and it suffered early from railway competition. Traffic stopped in 1906 and the canal was formally abandoned in 1914.

BOAT TRIPS

Charlotte Dundas This paddle-driven boat, operated by the Kennet & Avon Canal Trust runs pleasure trips on the long pound, between Devizes and Pewsey. Details from: Bookings Manager, Calcote, Bath rd, Devizes. (5550).

PUBS

Kings Arms All Cannings. ¼ mile S of Woodway Bridge.

Barge Honey st. Canalside. Caravan hire. (Woodborough 238).

✕ **White Bear** Market Place, Devizes. (2444). This 18thC coaching inn has a French and English restaurant. Many other pubs and restaurants in Devizes.

New Inn Coate. Beer garden, with a small aviary of exotic birds.

Crown Bishops Cannings. Snacks.

Bridge Inn Horton. Canalside, by Horton Bridge. B&B.

Brewery Inn Seend Cleave. ¼ mile from lock 19.

Bell Inn Seend. On A361. ½ mile from lock 21.

Barge Inn Seend. Canalside, by lock 19. Bar billiards. PO box.

Three Magpies Sells Green. On A365, ¼ mile from Martinslade Bridge.

Black Horse Inn Lock 48, Caen Hill, Devizes.

Somerset Arms Semington. ¼ mile S of Semington Bridge.

The Caen Hill Flight, on the Kennet & Avon, now being restored. *Derek Pratt.*

Bath

22½ miles (to Hanham Lock)

Continuing westwards the canal and the River Avon converge and run closely together all the way to Bath, parting only at Bradford where the canal keeps well above the town. The once dry section as far as the Avoncliff Aqueduct has been restored, with the assistance of the Manpower Services Commission. The canal crosses the Avon on the Dundas Aqueduct. At the other side is a small wharf and basin, which used to be the junction with the Somersetshire Coal Canal. The Canal maintains the level of the 9-mile pound that runs from Bradford to Bath Top Lock. The Widcombe flight of locks, although restored in 1976, cannot be used. The Avon is joined immediately beyond Bath Lock. The junction is the only point of access to Bath as a whole. Hanham Lock is the last lock between Reading and Bristol (except Netham Lock 1 mile short of Bristol, operated by a P.O.B.A. Lock keeper) and the end of the BWB's jurisdiction. Note that the River Avon is tidal west of Hanham Lock. A canal takes boats through Bristol harbour; the navigation then rejoins the river which flows down to the Severn estuary at Avonmouth.

Navigating the Bristol Avon
Pleasure boats should always give way to barges, and should let them use the locks first. In general, downstream traffic has right of way, especially through bridges. All the locks are accompanied by weirs, and so boatmen should take great care to turn into the lock cuts, and avoid the weir channel. Remember that a river always has a current, and is liable to changes in speed and level of flow. When mooring, allow enough slack on lines. Do not moor in lock cuts or near weirs. All pleasure boats should moor up at night, and show a white light. With the exception of Hanham and Netham, the locks are not manned. Remember that boats should always be held by ropes while the locks are being operated, for there is a strong turbulence in these large locks.

Avoncliff
Wilts. Station. Originally a weaving centre. Dominated by Rennie's aqueduct, 1804.
Bradford on Avon
Wilts. Pop 7300. EC Wed. All services. A beauty spot, and one of the highlights of the canal. A weaving centre until the 19thC. Rich in architectural treasures. There is a swimming pool near the canal.
Bradford Wharf Some original buildings still stand. Plenty of mooring space.
Town Bridge The 9-arched bridge is unusual in having a chapel in the middle. Parts of the bridge, including the chapel, are medieval.
Holy Trinity Church Basically a 12thC building. Inside are some medieval wall paintings, and fine 18thC monuments.
Saxon Church of St. Lawrence Founded 705, this tiny church was enlarged in the 10thC. It survives practically unchanged.
Great Tithe Barn 14thC. Standing below the canal embankment, this is one of the finest tithe barns in England. Maintained by the Dept. of the Environment. *Open at most times*
Westwood Manor 1m SW of Bradford. 15thC stone manor house containing much original Jacobean plaster and woodwork. *Open Apr-Sep. Wed 14.30–18.00.*
Staverton
Wilts. Tel. stores. Terraces of weavers' cottages. A small isolated part of the river is navigable here, and is used by a few pleasure boats.
Hilperton
Wilts. PO, tel. stores, garage. Wyke House stands to the west of the village. This very ornate mansion, built in 1865, is a replica of the original house. *Not open to the public.*

Claverton
Avon. Tel. Peaceful manorial village surrounding the 17thC farm.
Claverton Manor Built 1820 in the Greek revival style, it now houses a museum of American decorative arts. *Open Apr-Oct. Tue-Sun. 14.00–17.00. Winter on application only.* (Bath 60503).
Claverton Pump The waterwheel pump is unique on British canals. Designed by John Rennie, it was built to feed the 9-mile Bradford-Bath pound and started operating in 1813. A major breakdown in 1952 prompted its closure and replacement by a temporary diesel pump. A complete renovation of the pump and machinery by Bath University now has water being raised 53ft from the Avon. *Open Sun*, and operating three or four weekends per year.

Dundas Aqueduct Built 1804. Stands as a fitting monument to the architectural and engineering skill of John Rennie.
Somersetshire Coal Canal Opened in 1805 as a means of moving coal to Bath, Bristol and the rest of England. Originally surveyed by Rennie in 1793, the canal was to run from Limpley Stoke to Paulton, with a branch to Radstock. Steep gradients plagued the canal throughout its life; it was never profitable and was sold to the Somerset and Dorset Railway in 1871. The canal was officially abandoned in 1904. *(See 'The Somersetshire Coal Canal and Railways' by K. R. Clew, published by David & Charles.)*
Limpley Stoke
Avon. PO, tel, stores. The little church includes work from all periods from Norman to the 20thC.
Freshford
Avon. PO, tel, stores, garage. Well worth the ½-mile walk S from Limpley Stoke. A particularly attractive village.
Bath
Avon. Pop 85,000. EC Thur. MD Wed. Extensive remains of the Roman spa town. In the medieval period it was the centre of the wool trade. But the true splendour of Bath is the 18thC development. Despite heavy bombing in the 1939–45 war, Bath is still a magnificent city.
Bath Abbey A pleasingly uniform perpendicular building, founded in 1499. Inside, the abbey is justly famous for its fan vaulting.
Holburne of Menstrie Museum Great Pultenay st (3669). Silver, ceramics and 18thC paintings and furniture. *Open: weekdays 11.00–13.00 and 14.00–17.00, Sun 14.30–17.30.*
Museum of Costume Assembly Rooms (28411). One of the largest displays of costume in the world. *Open daily.*
Bath Roman Museum Abbey Churchyard (28808). The great bath buildings and temple were the centre of Roman Bath. Much of these survive, incorporated into the 18thC Pump Room. The museum, attached to the bath buildings, contains finds excavated from the site. *Open: daily 09.00–18.00 (winter 17.00).*
1 Royal Crescent Typical mid-18thC house, complete with original furniture and fittings. *Open: Mar-Oct weekdays except Mon 11.00–17.00, Sun 14.00–17.00.*
Victoria Art Gallery Bridge st (28144) 18thC with modern paintings, prints and ceramics. Visiting exhibitions. *Open: weekdays 10.00–18.00, Sat 10.00–17.00.*
Bathampton.
Avon. PO, tel, stores, garage. Suburb of Bath. The church is mostly 19thC.
Swineford
Avon. PO, tel, stores.
Saltford
Pop 1700. EC Wed. PO, tel, stores, garage. Dormitory suburb of Bath.
Saltford Manor Situated by the church, one of the oldest inhabited houses in England. Original Norman work is hidden behind a 17thC façade.
Keynsham
Avon. All services. Suburb of Bristol. Remains of an Augustinian Abbey, founded 1170, in Abbey Park. The original 13thC church now has an attractive Victorian interior. Fine 16thC monument to Sir Henry Bridges.
Bitton
Avon. PO, tel, stores, garage. The splendid church has a long Saxon nave with Norman details, a 14thC chancel and a decorative late 14thC tower.

BOATYARDS & BWB

Ⓑ **Bristol Boats** by Saltford Lock. Jolly Sailor Boatyard. Mead lane, Saltford, Somerset (2032). [W] Boat building, sales and repairs, inboard and outboard engine sales and repairs. Slipway available. Chandlery. *Closed Sun.*
Ⓑ **Newbridge Boating Station** Newbridge rd, Bath. (24301). [R] [S] [W] Boat hire, slipway, gas, boat and engine repairs, mooring, chandlery, toilets, cafe, winter storage.
Ⓑ **Port Avon Marina** Bitton Road, Keynsham (61626). [R] [S] [W] [D] Slipway, gas, dry dock, boat and engine repairs, mooring, chandlery, toilets, winter storage.
BWB Hanham Lock (Keynsham 2550). River Registration Certificate – short and long term issues. 'Crash' licences available.

BOAT TRIPS

Waterbus Kingfisher Round trips in this 12 seater from Bath Top Lock to Bathampton on *Sat, Sun & B. Hols.* (Frome 830 360).
Ladywood 40 seater trip boat run by K & A Trust. (Bradford on Avon 6135).
Jane Austen carries passengers between Bathampton and Bath, offering scenic views of the city. For bookings contact Commander C. Wray-Bliss, Dundas Carrying Co. Easton House, Corsham (713149).
'The Bristol Packet' Wapping Wharf, Gas Ferry rd, Bristol (28157). Public trips on narrow boat *Redshank* and passenger steamer *Tower Belle*. Bristol Docks to Bath. (*Tower Belle* also to Avonmouth). *Easter to end Sept.*

PUBS & RESTAURANTS

Crossed Guns Avoncliff.
Barge Inn Bradford. Canalside, by wharf. Food. B&B. Tel 3403.
Canal Tavern Bradford. Canalside.
Kings Arms Hilperton. 100yds S of Hilperton Wharf.
Viaduct Hotel Claverton, on Bath rd, 200yds S of Dundas Aqueduct. B&B. Restaurant. (Limpley Stoke 3187).
Tearles Restaurant Limpley Stoke. Beside Avon Bridge. (Limpley Stoke 3150).
Hop Pole Limpley Stoke.
Plenty of pubs in Bath.
Priory Hotel Weston rd, Bath (21887). Comfortable and cordial. B&B. D only.
The Laden Table 7 Edgar Buildings, George st, Bath (64356). Good food at fair prices. Set lunch. *Closed Sun, Mon, B. Hols. Must book.*
George Inn Bathampton. Canalside.
Swan Swineford.
Jolly Sailor By Saltford Lock. Riverside garden.
Bird in Hand Saltford.
Chequers Inn Hanham. Riverside.
Le d'Avon Keynsham, by the lock. Food. Plenty of pubs in Keynsham.
White Hart Bitton. On A431.

Lee & Stort Navigations

Parts of the river Lee (or Lea) were used as navigations in Roman times, and much of the river was navigable before the reign of Elizabeth I. In 1571 an artificial cut was made and a pound lock was built at Waltham Abbey using two sets of mitred gates, a principle that became a standard feature of lock design. Since the 17thC, the Lee has been a source of water supply for London. The navigation was steadily improved throughout the 18thC and 19thC. Enlargements were carried out during and immediately after the 1914-18 war to allow 130 ton boats to reach Enfield, and 100 ton boats to Ware and Hertford. In the 1930's further canalisation was carried out and more recently locks have been mechanised and duplicated. The timber trade of the Lee navigation survives today.

The River Stort, whose navigation dates back over 200 years, has never been very significant commercially. It has been owned by a series of individuals and companies including Sir George Duckett.

A rapidly increasing population needs an area of open space in which to enjoy its leisure time. The Lee Valley Regional Park Authority was set up to turn the Lee valley into a regional park which extends from Eastway (A106) to Ware. It aims to cater for all ages and tastes with many indoor and outdoor activities.

River Lee
LIMEHOUSE BASIN to
Enfield Lock: 13 miles, 6 locks
FEILDE'S WEIR (junction with river Stort): $20\frac{1}{2}$ miles, 14 locks
HERTFORD, head of navigation, $27\frac{3}{4}$ miles, 18 locks

River Stort
FEILDE'S WEIR (junction with river Lee) to
Harlow lock: $6\frac{3}{4}$ miles, 8 locks
BISHOPS STORTFORD, head of navigation: $13\frac{3}{4}$ miles, 15 locks

Maximum dimensions
Limehouse Basin to Old Ford—Length 87', Beam: 19', Headroom: 8'.
Old Ford to Enfield lock—Length: 85', Beam: 18', Headroom: 6' 9".
Enfield lock to Hertford—Length: 85', Beam: 15' 9", Headroom: 6' 9".
River Stort—Length: 85', Beam: 13' 3", Headroom: 5' 9".

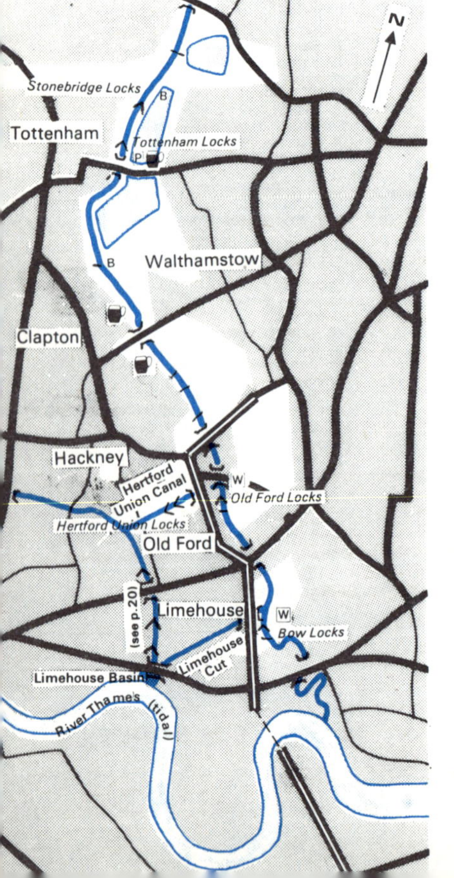

$9\frac{1}{2}$ miles

Most of the commercial (barge) traffic on the Lee is concentrated at the south end, below Enfield, and comprises mainly timber and copper. Barges are usually towed in trains of 2, 3 or 4 by a tug, so they have limited control over their steering and swing out across the river. Pleasure boat steerers must be very careful and keep a sharp lookout. It is particularly inadvisable to tie up on the outside of a bend. The rule of the river is of course, 'keep to the right'. Floating rubbish is another hazard in the vicinity of Limehouse Basin and Bow Locks. Taking a line ashore and 'bow hauling' may be necessary.

Entrance to the river navigation can be made from three places.

From Regent's Canal via the Hertford Union Canal.
From the Thames via Limehouse Basin.
From the Thames direct up Bow Creek, and through Bow locks.

The Hertford Union Canal is a short ($1\frac{1}{4}$ miles) canal built in 1830 by Sir George Duckett as a useful junction between the Regents Canal and the Lee navigation. The locks are open only during normal working hours, except on certain weekends. Full details available from BWB Licensing Office at Watford (26422). (Do *not* confuse these with Old Ford Locks on the Lee, only 2 miles away), a lock-keeper will see you through the 3 locks on the Hertford Union, or Duckett's, as it's more usually called. Note that this canal is prohibited to walkers and cyclists, except by permit.

The western entrance to Duckett's is very easy to pass without noticing. It is just below Old Ford Locks and looks like a private dock entrance.

The most direct route up into the River Lee from the Thames is through the ship lock into Limehouse Basin ($1\frac{1}{2}$ miles below Tower Bridge), then east through the new short cut and along the Limehouse Cut to Bow Locks and Old Ford. The ship lock is opened only during the 3 hours preceding high tide. More information on opening times can be obtained from the Dock-master's office at 01-790 3444.

The other entrance to the Lee navigation is by way of Bow Creek, whose mouth is 5 miles down the Thames from the Limehouse Basin entrance. Bow Creek is a tidal river it is in fact the mouth of the River Lee. It is very twisting, 2 miles long and only navigable around high tide. For information on this water, ring British Waterways at Bow Locks (01-987 5661). Bow Locks, which are tidal, are at the top of the creek where it joins the Limehouse Cut. They are opened for approximately 4 hours before and 2 hours after high tide. The Three Mills at Bow still remain from the 18thC, although they were modified some years later. Nearby is the Abbey Mills Pumping House of Gothic-Byzantine style designed in 1868 by Bazalgette, who was also responsible for the Thames Embankments. Beyond Hackney the river follows a wide, sweeping course northwards, becoming bleak and stark. It is inadvisable to venture up any of the side creeks; they are usually heavily silted. All the locks are operated by lock-keepers. The Old Copper Mill, Walthamstow (c.1800) ½m NE of Springfield boatyard, may be visited by parties. Contact Thames Water Authority, Roseberry avenue, London EC1 (01-837 3300).

Walthamstow Reservoirs alongside the east bank of the navigation: an important part of London's water supply, controlled by the Thames Water Authority. Access is allowed for bird-watching and fishing by permits obtained from the TWA, New River Head, Roseberry avenue, London EC1 (01-837 3300).

BOATYARDS & BWB

Ⓑ **Page & Hewitt** Marsh lane, Stonebridge Locks, London N17 (01-808 9013). RSWD Boat hire, slipway, gas, boat building and repairs, mooring, toilets, showers, winter storage. Trip boat for private charter.
Ⓑ **Springfield** Springhill, Clapton. (01-806 1717). RSWD Slipway, gas, boat and engine repairs, mooring, toilets, winter storage. *Closed weekend afternoons.*

PUBS & RESTAURANTS

Ship Aground Lea Bridge rd (A104). Canalside. Food.
Prince of Wales Lea Bridge. Canalside. Food.
✕ **Good Friends** 139 Salmon lane E14. (01-987 5541). Famous Chinese food.
✕ **Cook's Ferry Inn** Edmonton. Canalside. Food.
✕ **Ferry Boat Inn** Tottenham locks, Tottenham. Food.
Robin Hood Upper Clapton, opposite Walthamstow Marshes. Food.
Anchor & Hope Upper Clapton, opposite Walthamstow Marshes. Food.

Waltham Abbey

18 miles

The river passes Pickett's Lock, and is accompanied for nearly 4 miles by the King George & William Girling reservoirs to Enfield Lock. The canal now enters a market gardening area, followed by 5 miles of wilderness which will eventually be turned into a massive water parkland. The Broxbourne area, popular with holidaymakers, is busy with boats and fishermen in the summer. At Feilde's Weir the beautiful river Stort flows in from the north east, and the Lee bears north west to Stanstead Abbots, becoming smaller, shallower and more attractive. Boatmen should be careful when ascending Stanstead Lock: the top paddles are unusually on the gates; the unexpected rush of water into the lock chamber can cause great harm to the unprepared. The river now runs north west by water meadows, turning west into Ware 'The Granary of London'. Ware Lock is beautifully maintained by the Thames Water Authority. The river wanders on to Hertford, entering the town by a deep lock. A weir in the centre of the town prevents further progress.

Chingford
Essex. All Saints church is medieval. On a 300ft hill to the north of the town, 1½m from Ponders End Locks, is a pole obelisk erected in 1825 as a North mark for Greenwich Observatory. 1m E of the obelisk is Queen Elizabeth I's Hunting Lodge, housing a museum. Epping Forest, remarkable for its hornbeams and deer, lies NE of Chingford.
Enfield
Middx. The church of St Andrew in the market place has a 13thC chancel window. Gentlemen's Row (early 18thC), is completely preserved from numbers 9-23.
Waltham Cross
Herts. Pop 10,460. EC Thur. All services. The Eleanor Cross, built 1291, restored in the 19thC, is 1m W along the A121. It is one of the 12 crosses erected by Edward I to commemorate his dead queen's last resting places on her journey to Westminster Abbey.
Waltham Abbey
Essex. Pop 13,790. EC Thur. All services. King Harold chose the town for development as a centre of learning and religious instruction.
Abbey Church Founded in 1030. Nominated a mitred abbey in 1184. Today's building is mostly 19thC, but the Norman nave and aisle still stand. Fine Burne-Jones window (1861) at the east end.
Cheshunt
Herts. Pop 43,780. EC Thur. All services. Perpendicular church of St Mary's built 1414-48. There is a carnival every *Jul.*
Broxbourne
Herts. Pop 3840. EC Wed. All services. The church is entirely 15thC and 16thC. In the High street are several 17thC timber framed Georgian brick houses.
Hoddesdon
Herts. Pop 21,000. EC Thur. MD Wed. All services. A fair is held in *June.*
Rye House Plot It was in the Rye House that a group of conspirators plotted to ambush King Charles II and his son James, heir to the throne. The plot failed, and many of the traitors were put to death.
Stanstead Abbots
Herts. Pop 1460. EC Thur. All services. The church of St James has an interesting 15thC open timber south porch, and a 16thC brick north chancel chapel.
Ware
Herts. Pop 14,000. EC Thur. MD Tue. All services. There is much evidence of a former medieval town.
Ware Priory Priory st. Built from the remains of a Franciscan friary founded in 1338.
St Mary's Church Church st. Has a battlemented clock tower. A fascinating story is connected with the oak railings enclosing the children's corner.

The New River
Opposite Ware Park is the intake from the River Lee of the New River, which continues 24m S to Stoke Newington. It was a great engineering feat designed by Sir Hugh Myddelton in 17thC to bring fresh water from Amwell Springs (now run dry) to north London to replace the polluted supply obtained from the Thames. Work started on the remarkable plan in 1609 and the original course, including several large wooden aquaducts, was completed within 4 years. A monument to Myddelton's achievement can be seen on an island at the foot of the slope below Great Amwell church, ¼m W of the iron footbridge half way between Hardmead and Stanstead locks.

Hertford
Herts. Pop 19,080. EC Thur. MD Mon. All services. Two medieval parish churches still stand. The town centre is delightful.
The Castle Built in 1100, the castle has a rich history. It was here Bolingbroke drew up charges against Richard II which lead to his dethronement in 1399. A few medieval structures remain, including a 12thC curtain wall. There are several noteworthy buildings in Water lane and Castle street.
Hertford Museum 18 Bull Plain. Local interest. *Open daily.*

BOATYARDS & BWB

BWB Enfield Maintenance Yard Ordnance rd, Enfield lock. (Waltham Cross 22283/4).
Ⓑ **Broxbourne Boat Centre** Old Nazeing rd, Broxbourne (Hoddesdon 62085). Near Broxbourne Station. [S] Day boat hire, trip boat charter, Slipway. *Closed winter.*
Ⓑ **Hayes-Allen Boatyard Co** Rye House Quay, Rye rd, Hoddesdon (60888). [R] [W] [D] Day boat hire, slipway, mooring, chandlery, toilets, provisions, winter storage, engine sales and service.
Ⓑ **Hazelmere Marine** Highbridge st, Waltham Abbey (Lea Valley 711865). [R] [S] [W] Slipway, repairs, mooring, toilets. *Closed weekends.*
Ⓑ **Lea Valley Narrow Boat Co** Victoria Malting, Broadmeads, Ware (3626). [W] [D] Pump-out. Narrow boat hire, gas, boat building and repairs, chandlery. Some public trips and private charter.

PUBS & RESTAURANTS

- **Greyhound** Enfield Lock. Canalside. Food.
- **Royal Small Arms** Enfield Lock. Canalside. Food, snooker table.
- **Railway** Ponders End Station.
- **Old English Gentleman** Waltham Town Lock. Canalside. Food.
- **Jolly Fisherman** Stanstead Abbots. Canalside. Food.
- ✕ **Rye House** Canalside. Food
- **Fish & Eels** Dobbs Weir, Broxbourne. Canalside. Food.
- **Crown Inn** Broxbourne. Canalside. Food.
- **Woolpack** near Mill bridge, Hertford. Food.
- ✕ **Salisbury Arms Hotel** Fore st, Hertford. (3091). Food.
- ✕ **White Hart Hotel** Salisbury square, Hertford. (3615). Food.

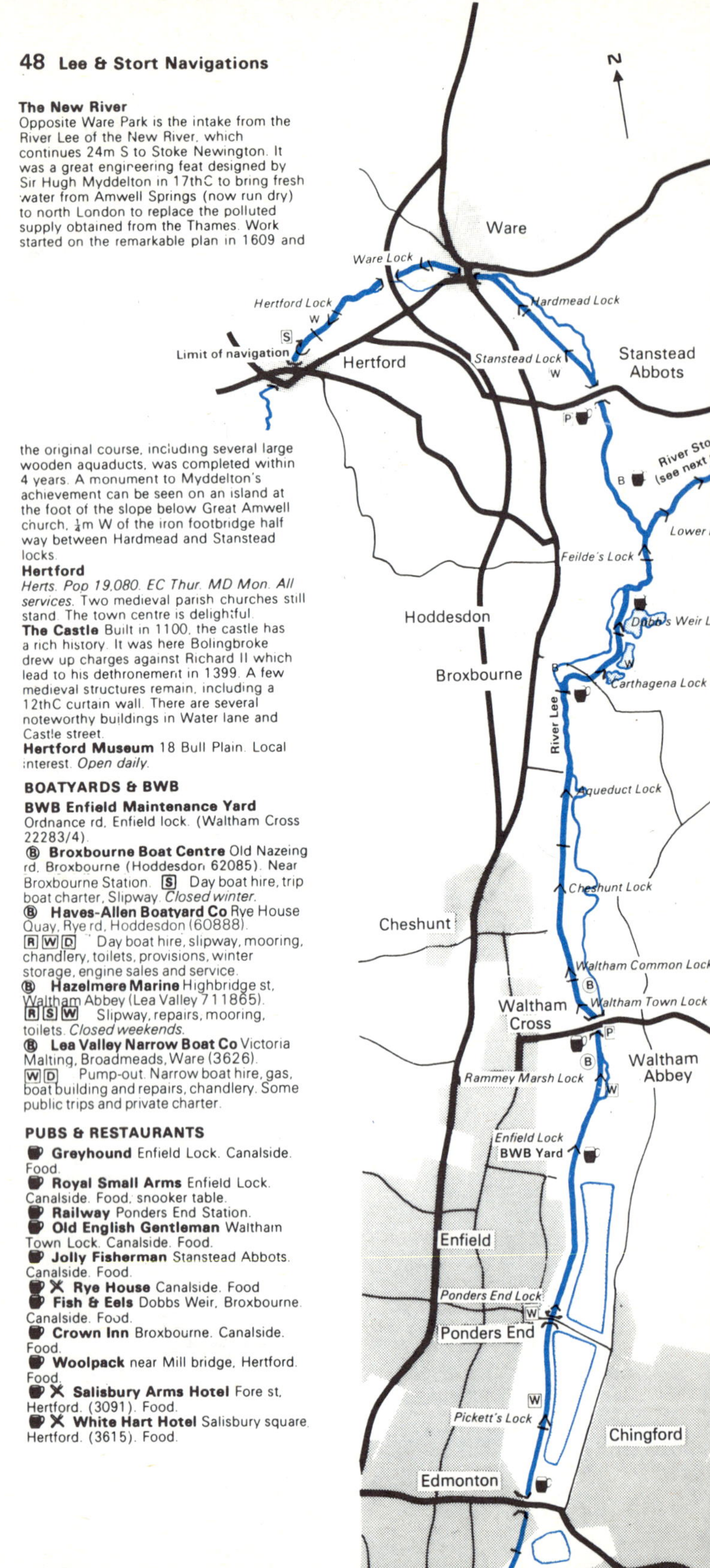

Bishops Stortford

13¾ miles

North east of Feilde's Lock, the Stort passes Roydon Mill and comes to Roydon Lock which must always be left empty to avoid flooding the lock-keeper's cottage. At Sheering Mill Lock, the water point is at the back of the lock cottage. The river continues into Bishops Stortford. Do not attempt to go beyond the point where it divides. You will probably get stuck.

Roydon
Essex. Pop 2830. EC Wed. PO, tel, stores, station. The church dates from the 13thC.
Harlow
Essex. Pop 74,110. EC Wed. MD Tue/Fri/Sat. All services. The Old Town contains several 18thC houses, a Norman chapel at Harlowbury and the site of a Romano-Celtic temple.
Harlow Town Pets' Corner Harlow Park. Animals roaming free. Aquarium, vivarium and aviaries. *Open daily.*
Parndon Mill at Parndon Lock, Harlow. (20982). Watermill housing arts and crafts centre. *Open Sat & Sun.*
Sawbridgeworth
Herts. Pop 6310. EC Thur/Sat. All services. The large 14thC and 15thC church is rich in monuments and brasses. Many attractive white clapboarded buildings.
Hyde Hall E of the Stort, 1m from town centre. Tudor style mansion built 1806.
Pishiobury Castellated mansion rebuilt in 1782. Tudor and Jacobean work inside. Park and lake by Capability Brown.
Little Hallingbury
Essex. Pop 1020. PO, tel, stores. The church has a Norman doorway made with Roman bricks.
Thorley
Herts. The church retains its Norman south doorway and a west tower from the 15thC. Extensively restored 1854.
Bishops Stortford
Herts. Pop 21,270. EC Wed. MD Thur. All services. Many old inns. St Michael's church has a Norman font surviving from an earlier church built on the same site.
Rhodes Memorial Museum. South rd. Contains a collection illustrating Cecil Rhodes' life.
Waytemore Castle Bridge st. Only the foundations of the keep remain.

BOATYARDS & BWB

Ⓑ **Lee & Stort Cruises** Little Hallingbury Mill, Bishops Stortford. (Bishops Stortford 384619). [R] Gas, dry dock, boat and engine repairs, mooring, toilets. 54 seat passenger boat available for charter.

BOAT TRIPS

Charter day trips from Little Hallingbury Mill. Bar on board. Meals arranged. Enquiries to Bishops Stortford 723568.

PUBS & RESTAURANTS

New Inn Roydon. Food.
White Hart Roydon. Food.
Straw Hat Restaurant London rd, Sawbridgeworth. (Bishops Stortford 722434). *Closed Mon; Sun D.*
King William IV Fairgreen, Sawbridgeworth.
Old Bell Sawbridgeworth. Good food.
Mill House Harlow Lock. (27156). Canalside. Restaurant.
Churchgate Hotel Churchgate st, Harlow. (21544). Food.
Dusty Miller ½m N of Burnt Mill Lock. Food.
Dane House Hotel Hadham rd, Bishops Stortford. (2289).
Foxley Hotel Stansted rd, Bishops Stortford. (4679). Locally popular.
Tanners Arms Station rd, Bishops Stortford. Canalside. Food.

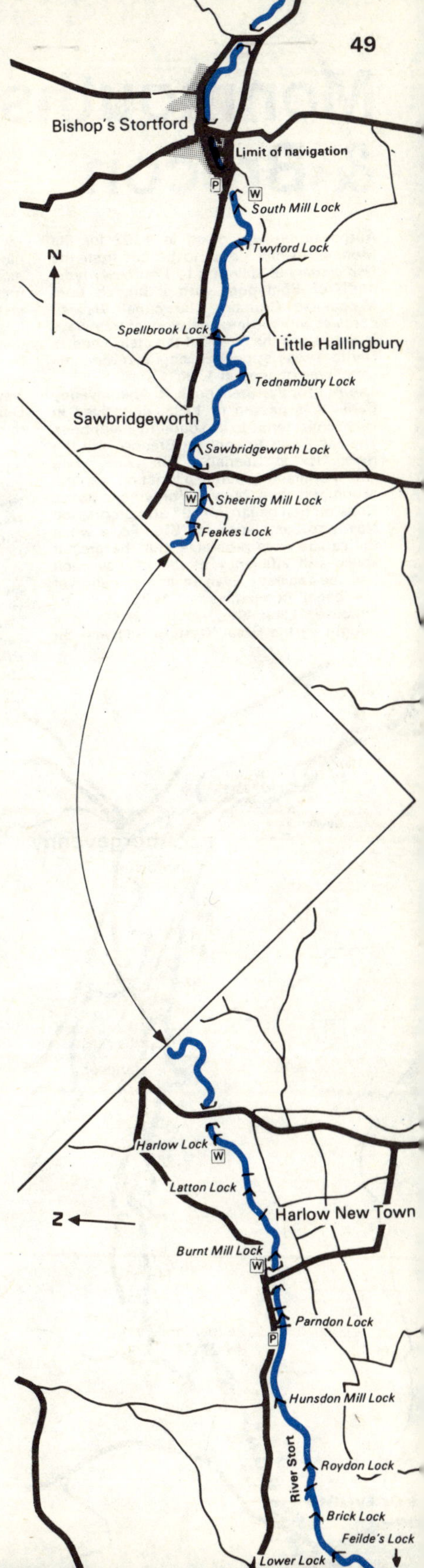

Monmouthshire & Brecon

Authorisation was given in 1792 for the Monmouthshire Canal to be cut from the Usk estuary at Newport to Pontnewynydd, north of Pontypool with a branch from Malpas to Crumlin. The canal was to connect with the large network of tramways built to serve the mines of the area. Thomas Dadford was appointed engineer, and the canal was opened in 1796.

The Act for the Brecknock & Abergavenny Canal was passed in 1793, conceived in very similar terms to its southerly neighbour. The canal was to connect Brecon with the River Usk at Caerleon. The plans were later modified to include a junction with the Monmouthshire Canal at Pontymoile Basin. Construction began in 1797 and progressed slowly to completion in 1812. For a while the canals were profitable, but the greater speed and efficiency of the railway soon became apparent. Even an amalgamation of the canal companies in 1865 was ineffective. Later the whole system was bought by the Great Western Railway. Bit by bit the Monmouthshire Canal was closed, but the Brecon line was kept open as a water channel. The network was finally abandoned in 1962. However, restoration work was started on the Brecon line in 1964. In 1970 a new lift bridge installed at Talybont made Brecon once more accessible to boats. Restoration is now in hand on the main line north of Newport, and also on the Crumlin branch. Despite several major obstacles, it is hoped through navigation will one day be possible.

Maximum dimensions
Length: 55′
Beam: 8′6″
Headroom: 5′7″
Mileage
PONTYPOOL to
Goytre Wharf: 6
Llanfoist: 11½
Gilwern: 14½
Llangattock Bridge: 18
Talybont: 26½
BRECON: 33¼
Total 6 locks

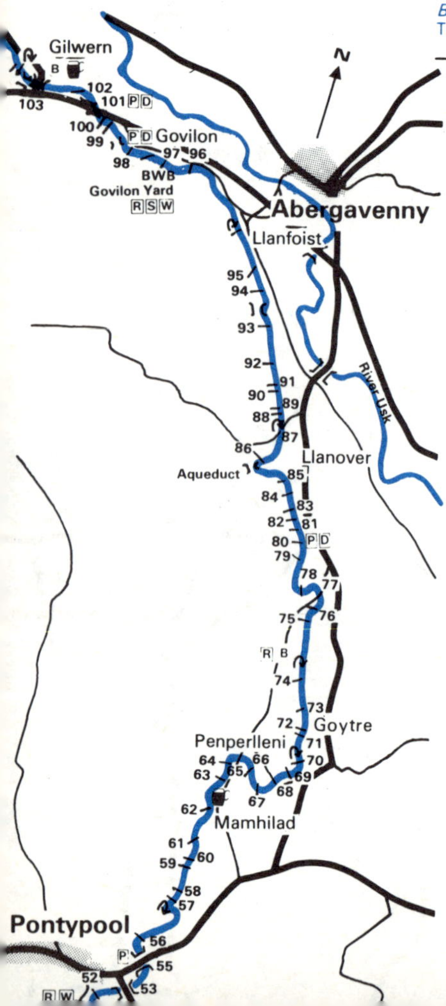

14½ miles

Although Jockey Bridge is the BWB official limit of navigation, the canal continues south to Crown Bridge in Sebastopol. Passing the turn-over bridge, toll house and site of the stop lock that marked the junction with the southerly section, the canal turns north-east and twists and turns up the Usk valley. The frequent stone bridges are all clearly numbered, and navigators should look out for the cast iron mile posts that survive irregularly along the length of the canal. Despite a lack of villages, services and pubs are never more than a short walk away. Passing the attractive Goytre Wharf, the canal maintains its level high on the side of the hills, at times making horseshoe bends and passing on an aqueduct over a rushing stream below. The River Usk approaches the canal, its course into Abergavenny being visible below. Traces of the old tramways that carried coal, iron and limestone down to the canals can still be seen—a good example leaves the canal by the boathouse at Llanfoist.

Penperlleni
Gwent. PO, tel, stores, garage.
Mamhilad
Gwent. Tel, stores. Hillside hamlet.
Pontypool
Gwent. Pop 37,000. EC Thur. MD Wed, Fri, Sat. An iron producing town since Roman times. The industry reached a peak in the 18thC and 19thC and has since declined. The town has also been famous for tinplating, japanning and coal mining. However, Pontypool has also remained a farming centre and market town.
Pontypool Park Georgian mansion, originally the seat of the Hanburys, the famous iron and steel family. The magnificent wrought iron entrance gates were presented by Sarah Churchill, Duchess of Marlborough. *Open to the public.*

Abergavenny
Gwent. Pop 9600. EC Thur. MD Tue. All services. 'The gateway to Wales'.
Primarily a market town, it contains buildings of all periods and styles, from Tudor to 19thC Gothic.
Abergavenny Castle The mound of the 11thC castle dominates the town. Site of a treacherous massacre in 1177. Ruins and grounds *open daily*.
St. Mary's Church Originally the chapel of the Benedictine Priory. Contains fine 14thC choir stalls, wooden figure of Jesse and rich monuments in the Herbert chapel.
Abergavenny and District Museum Castle precincts. Local interest. *Open daily*.
Sugar Loaf 2m NW of Abergavenny. A conspicuous 1955ft landmark owned by The National Trust.
Rural Crafts Museum Llanvapely, 4m E of Abergavenny, on B4233. Farming and domestic tools and implements. *Open Sun only 15.00–18.00.*
Llanellen
Gwent. PO, tel, stores. Attractive village, now a suburb of Abergavenny.
Llanover
Gwent. PO, tel, garage. The estate village is particularly elegant; stone cottages and terraces built in the same style.

BOATYARDS & BWB

O. T. Wrintmore Great House Farm, Goytre, Pontypool. (Little Mill 247). Day boat hire.
Ⓑ **Red Line Boats** Goytre Wharf, Pontypool, Gwent. (Nantyderry 880516).
RSWPD. Boat hire, slipway, gas, dry dock, boat building and repairs, mooring, chandlery, toilets, showers, provisions, winter storage. 20 seater trip boat.

BOAT TRIPS

Owain Glyndŵr 46 seater water bus operated by S & M Charters and based at bridge 76 near Goytre. They have another boat based on Brynich, pulled by the steam tug 'Sarah Siddons'. (Raglan 690201).

PUBS

Goytre Arms Penperlleni. (376). ¼m E of bridge 72. Food.
Star Mamhilad. 200yds E of bridge 62.
Horse & Jockey Pontymoile, on A472 100yds E of bridge 55.
✕ Clarence Hotel Pontypool. (3050). Food. B&B. Plenty of pubs in Pontypool, also fish and chips.
Hen & Chickens Abergavenny. 1¼m E of canal between bridges 95 and 96. Plenty of pubs and restaurants in Abergavenny.
Goose & Cuckoo Llanover. Off the A4042.

Brecon

18¾ miles

The canal continues northwards, following its contour cut in the steep sides of the hill. Abergavenny is easily reached on foot from the boatyard bridge at Llanfoist and by car from Govilon Wharf. The canal passes above Gilwern and enters a quiet, wooded stretch. Llangattock is best approached from bridges 114 and 115. Llangattock Wharf makes a good base for exploring the Brecon Beacons. Approaching Llangynidr, the canal enters open rolling pastureland beside the Usk.
Bridge 129 is the best access point for the village. The small settlement by bridge 131 includes a shop, telephone, tennis courts and garage. The canal now reaches the Llangynidr flight of 5 locks which end the 23 mile-long pound. On the old wharf beyond the second lock is a toll house now used by the BWB; there is a water point and rubbish bins. The canal continues to Talybont. At the end of the village is an electrically operated lift bridge; instructions are clearly posted. The 3 conventional lift bridges that follow may be in the open position to stop livestock crossing the canal. Boatmen should always leave them as they find them. Beyond Penkelli, a long horseshoe bend passes Llanfrynach at some distance. Llanhamlach, which lies across the Usk, can be approached by the footbridge just north of bridge 160. In addition to its 13thC church, the area is rich in prehistoric remains. After the last lock, restored in 1970, the canal goes straight to Brecon, ending in a new basin just beyond bridge 166. A big brick warehouse dated 1892 marks the old head of navigation.

Gilwern
Gwent. PO, tel, stores. Fine views.
Govilon
Gwent. PO, tel, stores, garage. Steps lead down to the village from the aqueduct. Once a small industrial centre. Now quiet.
Llanfoist
Gwent. PO, tel, stores, golf course. Good walk from the boathouse, following the old tramway into the mountains.
Llangattock
Powys. PO, tel, stores. Once famous for weaving and lime kilns. The hills behind the village are riddled with limestone caves and quarries. One cave, Agen Allwedd, has 11 miles of underground passages: the entrance is in the Craig-y-Cilau nature reserve. For access, follow the course of the old tramway west from bridge 114. Permits to enter must be obtained in advance from: Cave Management Committee, 10 Elms rd, Govilon, Gwent. Permits for rock climbing, and for specimen collecting, must also be obtained from: Nature Conservancy, Plas Gogerddan, Aberystwyth, Dyfed.
Crickhowell
Powys. Pop 1370. EC Wed. MD Thur. PO, tel, stores, garage, bank. The road down through Llangattock leads to this fine market town with its 13-arch medieval stone bridge over the Usk. In the centre are the scant remains of a Norman castle. The 14thC church contains interesting stained glass.
Cwm Crawnon
Powys. Hamlet with famous pub. (See below.)
Tretower Court and Castle
Powys. 2½m NW of Crickhowell on A479. Ruins of late 14thC fortified manor house, built to replace a Norman castle whose remains still exist nearby.
Llangynidr
Powys. PO, tel, stores. Farming village scattered around pretty 19thC church.
Penkelli
Powys. PO, tel, stores. Once head of a medieval lordship. The castle mound remains.
Talybont
Powys. PO, tel, stores, garage. Quiet holiday village with a busy livestock market.
Llangorse Lake
3½m N of Talybont, the largest natural lake in South Wales. 502 acres given over

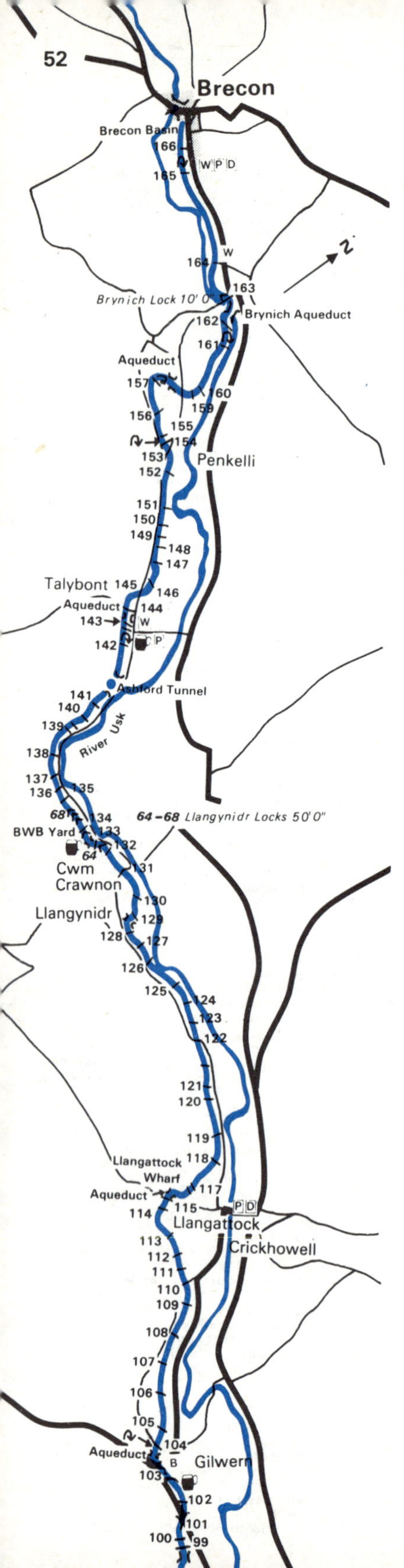

Brecon (cont)

to pleasure and recreation. Spectacular scenery, abundant wildlife. A lake dwelling set on stilts has been found near the lake's outlet.

Brecon
Powys. Pop 6300. EC Wed. MD Fri. PO, tel, stores, garage, bank, cinema, swimming pool. Has long been the administrative centre and market town for the surrounding uplands. It dates back to the Roman period, and the narrow streets that surround the castle give an idea of medieval Brecon. Now a famous touring centre.

Brecon Cathedral Originally the Priory church of St John, it was given cathedral status in 1923. Mostly 13thC. Fine glass.

Brecon Castle Permission to view the remains of the 11thC castle must be obtained from the Brecon Hotel in whose grounds most of them stand.

Brecknock Museum Glamorgan st. (Brecon 2218). Local interest. Includes a dugout canoe found in Llangorse Lake. *Closed Sun.*

Museum of the South Wales Borderers and the Monmouthshire Regiment The Barracks, Brecon. (3111). History of the regiments. *Open daily.*

Llanfrynach
Powys. PO, tel, stores. Attractive village and church. Nearby is the site of a Roman bath house. The pub dates from the 13thC.

BOATYARDS & BWB

Ⓑ **P. W. Coe** The Roadhouse, Gilwern, near Abergavenny, Gwent. (Gilwern 830240). R S D Boat hire, boat building and repairs, toilets, cafe.

Ⓑ **BWB Govilon Yard** (Gilwern 830328). R S W

Sovereign Marine Holidays Llangattock, Powys. The Booking Office, Lowesmoor Wharf, Worcester. (27022). Between bridges 114 and 115. Hire boats. Closed *Sat & Sun winter, Sun summer.*

BWB Llangynidr Maintenance Yard by bridge 134.

PUBS AND RESTAURANTS

Beaufort Arms Gilwern. Food, B&B.
Bridgend Gilwern.
Corn Exchange Gilwern. Food.
Navigation Gilwern. Canalside.
Lion Govilon, below aqueduct. Food.
Bridge Inn Llanfoist.
Llanfoist Inn Llanfoist.
Horse Shoe Llangattock. 20yds from bridge 116.
Bridgend Hotel Crickhowell (810338). Food, B&B.
✕ **Bear Hotel** Crickhowell (810408).
✕ **Coach & Horses** Cwm Crawnon, Llangynidr. (Bwlch 730245). Canalside. French cuisine.
✕ **Red Lion** Llangynidr. (Bwlch 730223). Food, B&B. Local trout and salmon served in 16thC surroundings. *Closed Sun.*
Star Inn Talybont. Canalside. B&B.
White Hart Talybont. Canalside.
Travellers' Rest Talybont. Canalside.
Many pubs and restaurants in Brecon.
Old Ford Llanhamlach. On A40, ½m cross-country from the canal. Food.
White Swan Llanfrynach, ¾m from bridges 158 or 157.

Oxford Canal

Authorised in 1769, this was the first canal linking London to Coventry and the Midlands to bring coal south from the Warwickshire coalfields. James Brindley was appointed engineer, and he designed a winding contour canal 91 miles long to join with the Thames at Oxford, where traffic could continue on to London. Brindley died in 1772, and work was continued under Samuel Simcock who saw the whole route opened to traffic in 1790. Although immediately successful, this was a tortuous route, and, when the Grand Junction opened a direct route from Braunston to London in 1805, this drew traffic away from the Oxford Canal. Only the outrageously high tolls charged by the Oxford Canal Company for the use of their 5½ mile stretch between Braunston and Napton protected their position.

However, the Oxford now looked outdated, so between 1829-34 a brave modernisation scheme was undertaken cutting 14 miles from the original 36 between Braunston and Coventry. This had the desired effect and the company remained profitable up to the 20th century.

Today the canal is quiet and sleepy with no trade. It passes through outstanding countryside and unspoilt villages.

Maximum dimensions
Length: 70′
Beam: 7′
Headroom: 7′

Main line
OXFORD (River Thames) to
Thrupp: 6½ miles, 4 locks
Lower Heyford: 14¾ miles, 9 locks
Aynho Wharf: 20¼ miles, 12 locks
Banbury: 27¼ miles, 17 locks
Cropredy: 31½ miles, 20 locks
Fenny Compton Wharf: 37¾ miles, 29 locks
Napton Bottom Lock: 47 miles, 38 locks
NAPTON JUNCTION (Grand Union Canal): 49¼ miles, 38 locks
BRAUNSTON TURN (Grand Union Canal): 54¼ miles, 38 locks
Hillmorton Bottom Lock: 61¾ miles, 41 locks
Stretton Stop: 70 miles, 41 locks
HAWKESBURY JUNCTION (Coventry Canal): 77 miles, 42 locks

5 miles

The Oxford Canal can be reached from the Thames in two places; one, via Duke's Cut, is convenient but by-passes Oxford altogether; the other, via a backwater under the north end of Oxford Station to the canal at Isis Lock, is more enjoyable but features a railway swing bridge only a foot or two above the water. This bridge, which needs 4 railwaymen to open it, has been a notorious obstruction for years, but fortunately BR do not use the bridge much now and only close it to boats when they need to. *It is open every day except from 14.30-16.30.* Past this bridge, boats continue for 50 yards along the backwater and should then join the canal by turning sharp left up into Isis Lock. After passing several wharves the houses give way to industry, while Port Meadow lies to the west. At bridge 240 there is PO, stores and off-licence, also swings for children. The first of the typical Oxford Canal lift bridges appears, followed by Wolvercote where the canal starts the long climb up to the midlands. After a series of main road bridges, Duke's Cut branches off to the west to join a backwater of the Thames, and the canal runs through lightly wooded fields and meadows to Kidlington.
For detailed information on Oxford, including Pubs and Restaurants, see River Thames section (p 65).

Kidlington
Oxon. Pop 8514. PO, tel, stores, garage, cinema. An Oxford suburb. 17thC gabled almshouses by Sir William Morton and parts of an older village survive around the church. Access from bridge 228.

BOATYARDS & BWB

Ⓑ **Castle Mill Boatyard** Cardigan street, Oxford. (57432) South end of canal. [R][S][W][D] Pump-out. Boat hire, gas, boat building and repairs, mooring, chandlery, toilets, winter storage. *Closed Sun.*

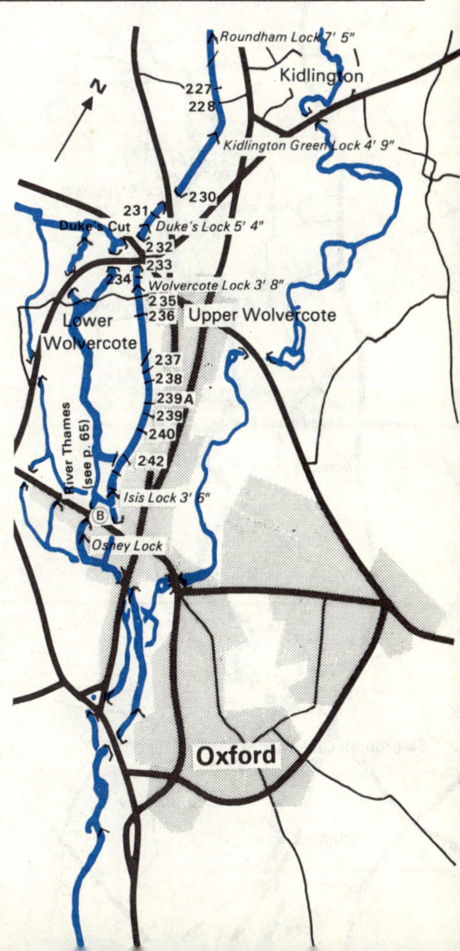

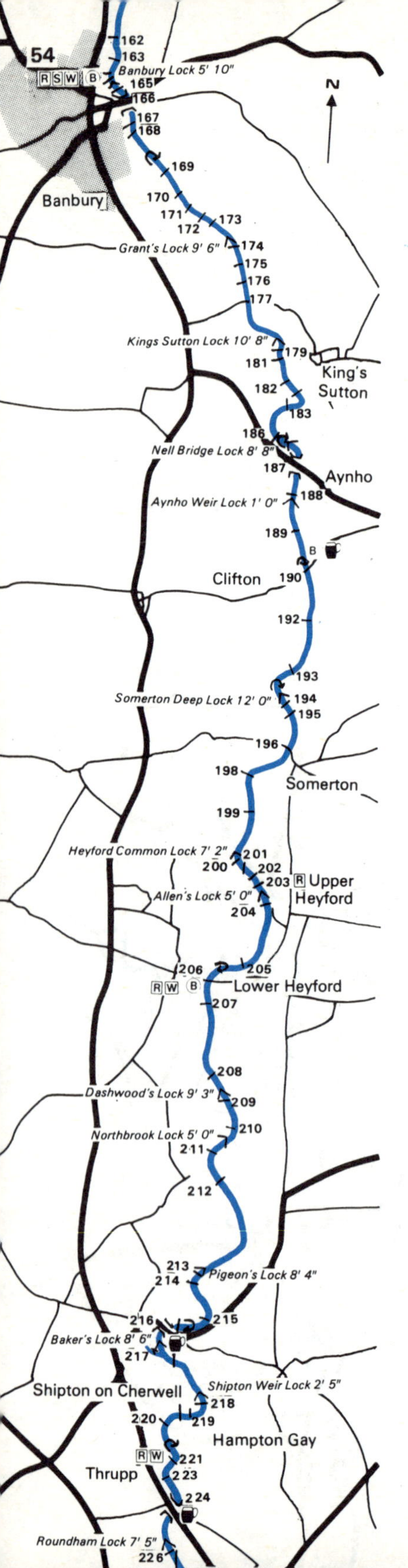

Lower Heyford

21½ miles

This is a delightful stretch of rural canal following the meandering course of the River Cherwell through fields, woods and water meadows. Most of the villages lie back from the canal, but at Thrupp and Lower Heyford wharves and warehouses reveal the canal's original purpose. The wooden lift bridges enhance its gentle and unobtrusive character.

Thrupp
Oxon. PO box, tel. A fine canal village alongside the towpath. An unusual survival of early canal prosperity.
Blenheim Palace *Oxon.* 3m W of Shipton at Woodstock. The English Versailles, built in 1722 by Sir John Vanbrugh. Sir Winston Churchill's birthplace. Fine furniture, paintings and tapestries.
Hampton Gay
Oxon. A deserted village, approachable only on foot (from bridge 220). Peace, seclusion and a ruined manor.
Shipton-on-Cherwell
Oxon. PO box. A magnificient situation; the wooded church overlooks the canal, the grey stone manor and farm overlook rolling fields.
Northbrook Bridge The stone canal bridge adjoins a much earlier packhorse bridge across the River Cherwell.
Rousham House Steeple Aston. Dates from 1635. Now enlarged; gardens landscaped 1730 by William Kent. Civil War associations.
Lower Heyford
Oxon. Pop 477. PO, tel, stores, station. Among woods on the south bank of the Cherwell. Church with fine stained glass. Ancient water mill and iron lift bridge.
Upper Heyford
Oxon. Pop 2190. PO, tel, store. Thatched stone cottages falling steeply to the canal while F-111's from the huge US air base roar overhead.
Somerton
Oxon. Pop 244. PO, tel, stores. A straggling grey stone village. Church with decorated tower.
Clifton
Oxon. PO, tel, stores.
Aynho
Northants. Pop 465. EC Tue. PO, tel, stores. 1m E of Aynho Wharf. Unchanged village square with rich stone. Aynho Park, a 17thC mansion rebuilt by Sir John Soane in the late 18thC. Fine paintings, furniture and Venetian glass.
Adderbury
Oxon. Contains one of the finest decorated and perpendicular style churches in the country with a 600-year-old spire.
King's Sutton
Northants. Pop 1550. PO, tel, stores, garage, station, pubs. An attractive village of narrow streets around a green. Access from br. 177.

BOATYARDS & BWB

Ⓑ **BWB Thrupp Yard** Kidlington (2222). R S W Moorings.
Ⓑ **K. Batty** Hilltop Cottage, Bletchingdon, Oxon. (366). W Slipway, moorings.
Ⓑ **Black Prince Narrow Boats** Canal Wharf, Lower Heyford. (40348). R S W D Pump-out. Boat hire, gas, dry dock, boat building and repairs, chandlery, toilets, provisions.
Ⓑ **Anglo Welsh Narrow Boats** Aynho Wharf, Banbury. (38483). R S W D Pump-out. Narrow boat hire, gas, boat and engine repairs, mooring, toilets, provisions, canal shop. *Facilities available Mon-Fri.*

PUBS

Boat Thrupp. Canalside, food.
Rock of Gibraltar Canalside at bridge 216. Food, garden, PO box.
Bell Lower Heyford. 16thC inn. Food.
Three Horseshoes Upper Heyford. Food.
Great Western Arms Aynho Wharf. Food. Playground. By Anglo-Welsh.

Banbury

23 miles

The canalside housing estates and industrial areas of Banbury soon give way to the more typical Oxford countryside as the canal continues its climb to the summit level at Claydon. Here it follows Brindley's extravagant 'contour' route after passing through the wooded cutting of 'Fenny Compton Tunnel'. At Marston Doles it starts its descent to meet the Grand Union at Napton Junction.

Banbury
Oxon. Pop 28,000. EC Tue. MD Thur/Sat. All services. Banbury is far more attractive than it appears from the canal. Originally a wool town, the castle was pulled down by Cromwell's forces in 1646. The ancient cross of nursery rhyme fame was pulled down in 1602, the present cross is a 19thC replica. The famous spiced Banbury cakes are still produced in the original bake house. See also the Museum and Globe Room.

Little Bourton
Oxon. PO box, tel, garage. Quiet residential village. *Stores* in nearby Great Bourton.

Claydon
Oxon. Pop 202. PO box, tel. An old fashioned brown stone village set in a rolling open landscape. Clattercote Priory, just to the south, still remains. The Claydon Granary Museum contains a fascinating array of relics, which you are welcome to handle, and is well worth the 1½m walk from the canal. There is also a small gift shop. Admission is free.

Cropredy
Oxon. Pop 459. PO, tel, stores, garage. A sleepy village of brick houses close to the canal. Stately sandstone church with fine woodwork. A plaque on the river bridge recalls the Battle of Cropredy, 1644.

Priors Hardwick
Warwicks. Pop 143. PO, tel. Approachable from the canal by footpath. A small village, partly deserted since it was pulled down by the Cistercian monks in the 14thC. Parts of the squat stone church are 13thC.

Wormleighton
Warwicks. Pop 190. PO, tel. A fine manorial village. Its 13thC brown stone church contains a perpendicular screen and Jacobean woodwork.

Fenny Compton
Warwicks. Pop 520. PO, tel, stores, garage. A scattered brown stone village. The church is partly 14thC and partly Victorian; alongside is a fine brick rectory of 1707. Fenny Compton Tunnel is no more, having been converted into a cutting in 1868.

Napton-on-the-Hill
Warwicks. Pop 760. PO, tel, stores, garage. Rising to over 400ft, Napton Hill dominates the immediate landscape, the village climbing steeply up the sides. The shops and pubs are at the bottom. Near the church, alone on the hilltop, is the recently restored windmill.

Marston Doles
Warwicks. Tel, stores. Tiny settlement that owes its existence to the canal. Nearby are the remains of the pumping house which used to pump water to the summit level.

BOATYARDS & BWB

Ⓑ **Cropredy Motor Cycles** by Cropredy Lock. (029-575 386). [W] Pump-out. *Mon-Sat.*

Ⓑ **Fenny Marine** Station Fields, Fenny Compton, Warwicks. (461/2/3). Large marina [R][S][W][P][D] Moorings, gas, chandlery, pump-out. Lavatories. Slipway, winter storage (hard standing). Manufacturers of steel narrow boats and 20 foot fibreglass boats. *Closed winter weekends.*

Ⓑ **Adkins Cruisers** Holt Farm, Southam, Warwicks. (Southam 2225). [R][S][W] Gas, moorings. *Closed winter.*

Ⓑ **A. J. Cruisers** 2 Market Hill, Southam, Warwicks. (Southam 2685). [R][S][W] Boat hire, gas, mooring, toilets, provisions.

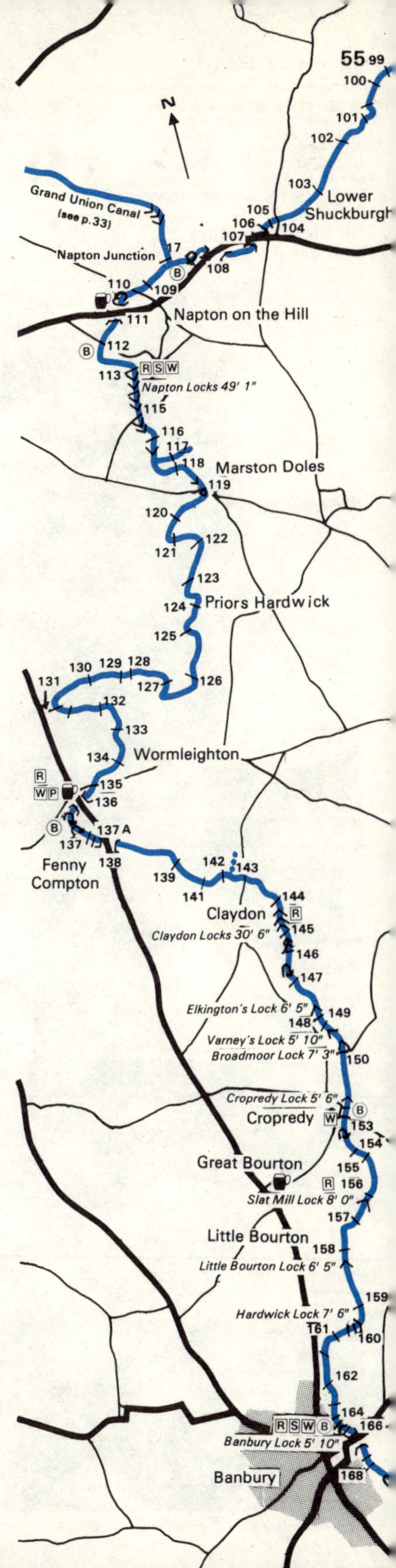

Ⓑ **Gordon's Pleasure Cruisers** Napton Marina, Stockton, Rugby, Warwicks. (Southam 3644). Steel hire cruisers [R] [S] [W] [D] Pump-out, gas, chandlery, launderette, showers. Slipway, covered wet dock. Moorings. Designers of steel narrow boats. Groceries available. *Open Apr-Oct.*

PUBS & RESTAURANTS

Plough Little Bourton. Food.

Swan Inn Great Bourton (Cropredy 8181).

Red Lion Cropredy. Food.

Brasenose Inn Cropredy (244).

Sunrising Claydon.

George and Dragon Fenny Compton Wharf (322). Canalside. Food *(except Sun)*. B & B, water.

Napton Bridge Inn Napton. (Southam 2466). Canalside. Lunches, dinners. Advisable to book.

Near Fenny Compton, Oxford Canal. *Derek Pratt.*

Braunston

15 miles

Leaving Napton, the Oxford Canal shares its route with the Grand Union to Braunston, then bears off to the north towards Rugby, the Grand Union continuing south east. This is open country, with evidence of medieval ridge and furrow field systems on the south bank; there are few villages and the landscape is quiet and empty. Approaching Rugby, radio masts can be seen to the east. The canal descends the three paired narrow locks and passes the attractively sited BWB maintenance yard at Hillmorton before swinging in a wide arc round Rugby.

Lower Shuckburgh
Northants. Pop 74. PO box. A tiny village along the main road. The church, built 1864, is very attractive. A farm, west of bridge 104, sells eggs.

Willoughby
Warwicks. PO, tel, stores, garage, cafe. A mellow red brick village. The small church is dominated by a fine 18thC rectory. Excellent home bakery.

Hillmorton
Warwicks. PO, tel, stores, garage. Its church dates from c.1300, with additions as late as 18thC. There is a medieval cross in the centre of the village.

BOATYARDS & BWB

Ⓑ **BWB Hillmorton Locks** Hillmorton. (Rugby 73149). R S W (D emergency only). Mooring, gas, toilets, dry dock, hire cruisers, pump-out. *Facilities Mon-Fri.*

Ⓑ **Rugby Boatbuilders** Hillmorton Wharf, Crick road, Rugby. (4438). S W D Steel narrow boats built, repaired or fitted out. Engines overhauled. Steel hire cruisers available. Gas, dry dock, mooring, chandlers, toilets, gift shop. *Closed winter Suns.*

Ⓑ **Clifton Cruisers** Clifton Wharf, Vicarage Hill, Rugby (3570). R S W D Pump-out. Boat hire, gas, repairs, toilets. *Phone first in winter.*

PUBS & RESTAURANTS

The Boatman Braunston (Rugby 890313). Popular canalside pub at Braunston Turn. Bar snacks, garden with swings. Meals *every day except Sun eve and all day Mon.*

Rose Inn Willoughby.

Stag and Pheasant Hillmorton. Food

Arnold Arms Barby (1¼ miles S of bridge 76). Food.

Rugby

13 miles

Swinging round Rugby, the canal enters a side cut embankment, then crosses the River Avon on an aqueduct. A short open stretch, then into Newbold Tunnel and a wooded cutting which gives way to fine farming land with small woods, some reaching to the water's edge. Past Brinklow the canal continues along an embankment (formerly an aqueduct, but now filled in) to Stretton before entering another deep cutting. The iron bridges that occur periodically mark the course prior to the 1829 shortening. Approaching Coventry the motorway makes its presence felt, and open land is replaced with pylons and housing. At Hawkesbury Junction, after some sharp bends, the Oxford Canal joins the Coventry.

Rugby
Warwicks. Pop 56,450. EC Wed. MD Mon/Sat. All services. Famous for the Rugby school where Rugby football was first played. The town was important for its agriculture for over 600 years, but today heavy electrical industries determine the character of the area. Visit the Library Exhibition Gallery and Museum, St Matthew st.

Newbold-on-Avon
Warwicks. PO, tel, stores, garage, fish and chips. A pleasant village with an interesting 15thC church. Near the tunnel mouth are two pubs right next door to each other—a fine sight.

Newbold Tunnel
This 250yd long tunnel was built during the shortening of the canal in the 1820's. The old tunnel mouth can be seen from the south by Newbold church.

Harborough Magna
Warwicks, PO, tel, stores. A quiet red brick village. 14thC church with interesting stained glass window.

Brinklow
Warwicks. Pop 1090. PO, tel, stores, garage. A spacious pre-industrial village built along a wide main street. The church is unusual in having a distinctly sloping floor.

Ansty
West Midlands. PO, tel, stores, garage. Tiny village that grew up along the canal. This area has been much altered by the motorway crossing to the south.

Shilton
West Midlands. PO, tel, stores, garage. Main road village left bewildered by the railway and the A46.

BOATYARDS & BWB

Ⓑ **Willow Wren Hire Cruisers** Rugby Wharf, off Consul rd, Leicester rd, Rugby. (4520). R S W P D Boat hire, gas, boat building and repairs, toilets. *Closed Sun.*

Ⓑ **Rose Narrowboats** Brinklow Marina, Stretton Stop. (Rugby 832449). R W P D Moorings, repairs, hire cruisers. Pump-out, gas, chandlery, provisions. Pottery made adjacent to the boatyard.

PUBS & RESTAURANTS

Three Horseshoes Hotel Sheep st, Rugby. (4585). Food.

Andalucia Restaurant 10 Henry st, Rugby. (76404). Good Spanish food. Book.

Golden Lion Harborough Magna. Food.

Boat Newbold Wharf. Canalside. Food skittles.

Barley Mow Newbold Wharf. Canalside. Food skittles.

White Lion Brinklow. Food.

Bull's Head Brinklow. Food.

Raven Brinklow. Food.

Railway Inn Stretton Stop. Canalside. Food.

Crown Shilton. Food.

Crown Ansty. Food.

Elephant and Castle Canalside. By bridge 4. Food.

Greyhound Hawkesbury Junction. Canalside. Food.

River Severn
Gloucester & Sharpness Canal

The River Severn has always been one of the principal navigations in England—at one time boats travelled as far as Welshpool. But with bigger boats the limit of navigation receded, and in the late 18thC the inland port of Bewdley was losing its significance. The opening of the Staffordshire & Worcestershire Canal in 1772 led to measures to improve the navigation, and as a result the Gloucester & Sharpness Ship Canal was completed in 1827. At the time of opening, this was the broadest and deepest canal in the world, a far sighted decision that has ensured the continued use of Gloucester and Sharpness Docks. The Severn Commission, formed in 1874, maintained the navigation of the Upper Severn. The ship canal still remains busy, but trade on the river above Gloucester has dwindled away. However, since the opening of the Upper and Lower Avon Navigations in 1974, the river is part of a fine circular cruising route, with the Worcester & Birmingham and the Stratford-on-Avon Canals completing the ring.

GLOUCESTER & SHARPNESS CANAL

Maximum dimensions
Length: 240′, Beam: 30′
Headroom: unlimited
Mileage
SHARPNESS Lock to
GLOUCESTER Lock: 16¾
Total 2 locks

RIVER SEVERN

Maximum dimensions
Gloucester to Worcester
Length: 135′, Beam: 21′
Headroom: 24′6″
Worcester to Stourport
Length: 90′, Beam: 19′
Headroom: 20′
Mileage
GLOUCESTER Lock to
TEWKESBURY junction with River Avon: 13
DIGLIS junction with Worcester & Birmingham Canal: 29
STOURPORT junction with Staffs & Worcs Canal: 42
Total 5 locks

---

10 miles

The Gloucester & Sharpness Ship Canal is the only navigable route between the Severn estuary and the Severn navigation at Gloucester, bypassing a dangerous tidal stretch of river. All boats heading upstream must pass through Sharpness Lock and Docks, and should time their arrival accurately, as the lock dries out at low water (the tidal range here is believed to be the second largest in the world). When locking down, arrive 2½ hours before high water, and about 1 hour before high water when locking up. Always give prior notice of your intentions to the BWB at Sharpness 228. Those who wish to navigate the Severn estuary are advised not to do so without a pilot.
Sharpness Docks, above the lock handle ships from Europe and Scandinavia, and pleasure craft are encouraged to move on through here to the canal without dawdling. After the two swing bridges a short arm leads west to a disused tidal basin—the arm itself is used for mooring, and there is a small boatyard at the end of it. The Forest of Dean can be seen across the estuary. A circular stone structure by the canal marks where a 22 arched railway bridge used to cross the river—it was damaged by a vessel in 1959 and demolished some time after. The canal is soon tree-lined and to the right are old timber ponds, where timber was stored afloat 'in the round'. The navigation then cuts through Purton, after which the landscape is predictably flat, with the mudflats and saltings of the estuary now much wider than at Sharpness, to the north.

Sharpness
Glos. Tel. stores and distant garage.
Sharpness exists only for its docks. It is situated on a wild and windy part of the estuary, facing the hilly Forest of Dean, and with an ever changing display of foreign ships. Here and there are rows of terraced cottages. The focus of the place is the lock (capable of handling ships up to 5000 tons).
Purton
Glos. PO, tel, stores. A tiny village bisected by the canal and dwarfed by the ships. There used to be a ford for cattle over the river—a treacherous crossing for the herdsman. A giant waterworks just outside the village

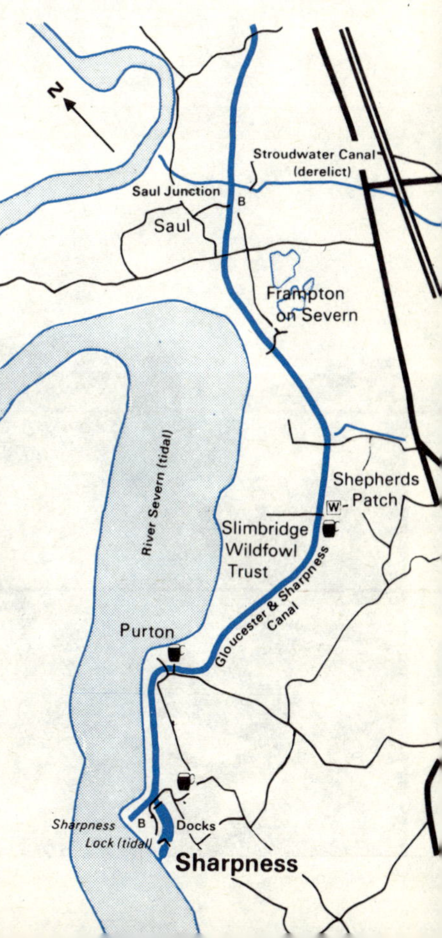

draws and purifies 24 million gallons of drinking water a day from the canal for Bristol.

Shepherds Patch

Shops, cafe, YHA. Where shepherds watched their flocks (grazing the Severn estuary). Just north of here is the:

Slimbridge Wildfowl Trust

One of the largest collections of captive wildfowl in the world (160 kinds), the Trust's grounds also attract many thousands of migrant birds, presenting a fascinating spectacle – from pink flamingoes to trumpeter swans (sounding not unlike elephants). Botanical and ecological study is carried out here, and the Trust has been responsible for saving several important species from extinction. *Open throughout the year except Christmas day.* Enquiries to Cambridge 333.

BOATYARDS & BWB

BWB Sharpness Office Dock Manager, Harbour Master and maintenance staff. (Dursley 348).

PUBS

Sharpness Hotel Sharpness. Haunt of the local 'ravers'.

Severn Bridge and Railway Sharpness. The pub sign recalls the now demolished bridge.

Berkeley Arms Purton. Excellent view of the Severn.

Berkeley Hunt Purton.

✕ **Tudor Arms** Shepherds Patch. Food.

Patch Hotel opposite the Tudor Arms.

Gloucester

13¾ miles

The surrounding land is flat and green with occasional trees. The Cotswolds can be seen to the east. The canal is punctuated with swing bridges, most of which have a dignified single storey bridge-keeper's cottage with fluted Doric columns and a pediment. Quedgeley Wharf is the northern-most point the oil traffic reaches; the barges no longer travel to Stourport. After Rea Bridge, industry replaces fields as the canal approaches Gloucester and its superb docks (check with the BWB Berthing Supt at Gloucester Lock Office if you wish to moor here). Gloucester Lock marks the end of the canal and lowers boats back into the Severn. From here follow the north channel upstream (Llanthory Lock to the SW is closed) onto a dull stretch of river. After the junction with the western channel, the river widens, and although the surrounding countryside is pretty, the navigator's view is obscured by trees and high banks. Landing is also difficult here.

Frampton on Severn

Glos. PO, tel, stores, garage. A beautiful linear village, with attractive houses spread along a green 100yds wide by a full ½ mile long, with trees and ponds. 14thC church with Romanesque lead font. Frampton Court (1731-33), a Georgian mansion with a Gothic Orangery.

Saul Junction

An unusual waterways 'crossroad' where the Stroudwater Canal crossed on its way from

Gloucester Docks.

the Thames & Severn Canal (both now disused) to the tidal Severn. A 300yd stretch to the SE is used for moorings. Restoration has started on both the Stroudwater and Thames & Severn Canals.

The Severn Bore
Best seen at Stonebench, Elmore, 500yds west of Lower Rea Bridge on the G & S. A 'tidal wave' flowing upstream on the Severn at certain states of the tide. SAE to Area Amenity Assistant, BWB Dock Office, Gloucester for annual predictions.

Navigational note: If your vessel can pass under certain bridges without their being opened, you *must* wait for the green light signal.

Gloucester
Pop 90,000. Street market Sat. Cattle market Mon & Thur. All services. Once the Roman town of Glevum (of which little remains), now a busy manufacturing town, commercial centre and port. The docks, built around 1827 are still handling cargo and have nine of the original seven storey warehouses still standing. **The cathedral** is essentially Norman but has fine examples of early perpendicular architecture. The great east window dates from 1350, and the cloisters feature the earliest known fan vaulting (mid-14thC). Visit also the City Museum & Art Gallery and the Folklife & Regimental Museum.

Ashleworth Quay
Glos. A fascinating group of 15thC buildings; Ashleworth Court, a church and a big stone tithe barn (still in use) behind the 'Boat' pub. Ashleworth Manor and the rest of the village are set well back from the river. Landing is difficult here–you may have to wade.

Navigational note: At Wainlode signs will be seen warning navigators to avoid the barges sunk here to prevent bank erosion.

BOATYARDS & BWB

BWB Gloucester Area Engineer's Office 27-29 Commercial Road, Gloucester (25524). Situated outside the docks not far from Gloucester Lock. The Berthing Superintendent on this number should be contacted by all boatmen intending to navigate the Ship Canal at weekends, night, early mornings and bank holidays. [W] beside the lock.

PUBS AND RESTAURANTS

- **Three Horseshoes** Frampton.
- **Bell Hotel** Frampton.
- **Castle Guest House** Canalside, at Park End Bridge. Lunch and dinner daily throughout the year. B&B. Groceries available [D] Enquiries and reservations to Hardwicke 328.
- **Anchor** Epney (on the river $1\frac{1}{2}$ miles west of Park End Bridge).
- **Pilot** Canalside, at Sellars Bridge.
- **Cross Keys** Gloucester.
- **Boat** Ashleworth. A delightful isolated pub on the river. Access is difficult (shallow water).

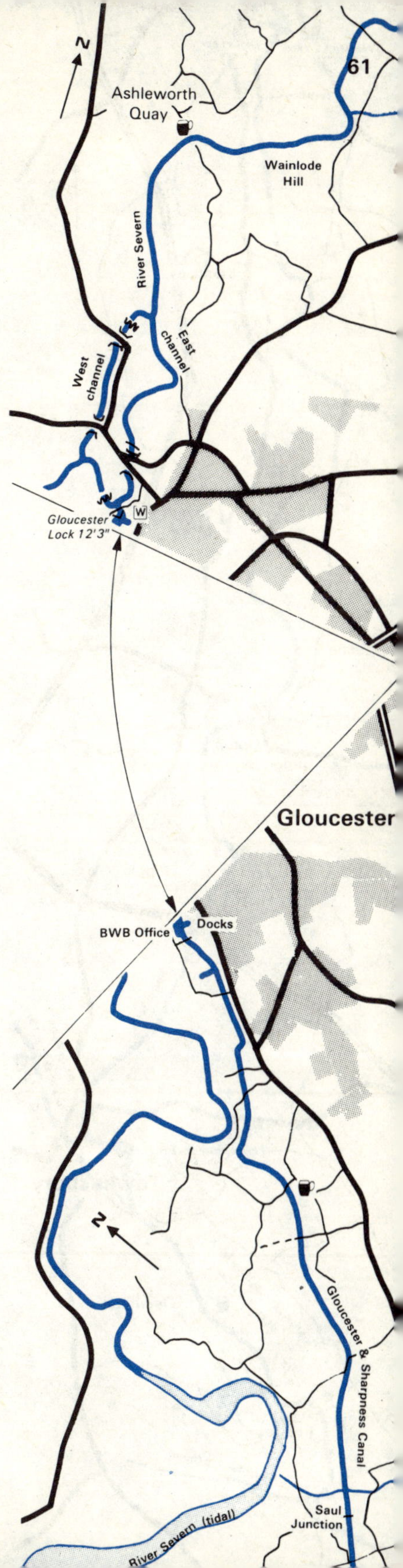

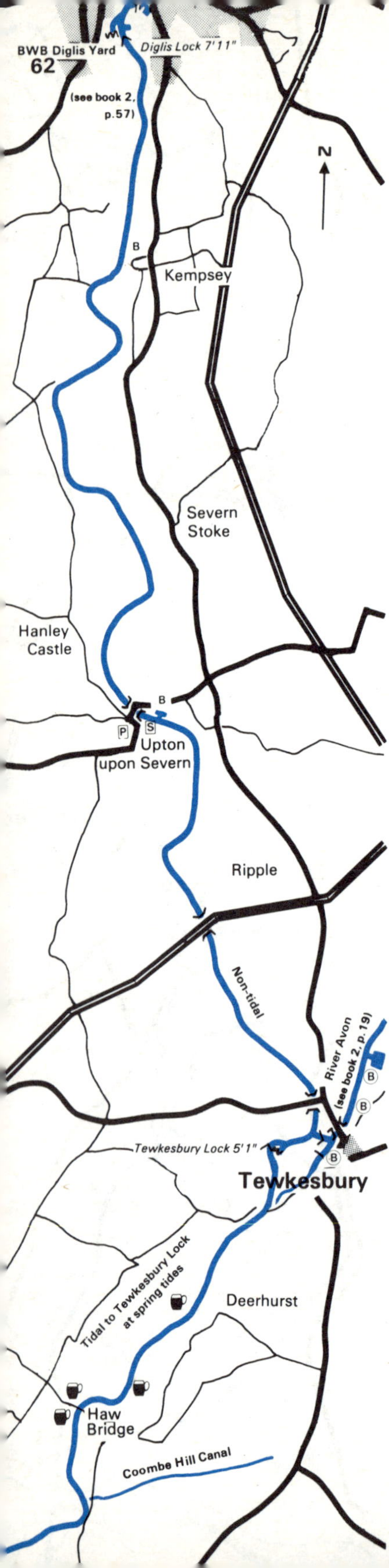

Tewkesbury

21 miles

Leaving Wainlode Hill behind, the river winds on to Tewkesbury where it is joined by the Warwickshire Avon. The river is tidal to here on spring tides. The town of Tewkesbury is separated from the river by a flat expanse of meadow, and navigators wishing to visit should proceed east up the Avon (entrance ABOVE Tewkesbury Lock). Above here the river resumes its usual character, isolated by high banks and trees until Upton upon Severn is reached with its interesting waterfront and many boats. Just west of Severn Stoke, tall red cliffs rise straight from the water, then caravans and bungalows appear interspersed along the banks as the river approaches Worcester where the Worcester & Birmingham canal leaves the river through Diglis Basin.

Deerhurst
Glos. Tel. stores. The beautiful church of St. Mary, parts of which date from 804, has one of the best preserved Saxon fonts in England. Odda's Chapel, 200yds SW of the church, is Anglo Saxon, dating from 1056. It was used as part of a farmhouse until rediscovered in 1885. Difficult access from the river over rocky banks.

Haw Bridge
Two pubs and a new bridge to replace the old one knocked down by a barge in 1958.

Coombe Hill Canal
Built in 1796 to carry coal to Cheltenham, and abandoned in 1876, it was recently purchased by the Severn & Canal Carrying Company at auction for £35,000. The 3 mile canal and its buildings are being restored to their original state.

Tewkesbury
Glos. Pop 8500. EC Thur. MD Wed. Sat. All services. Historic town at the junction of the Rivers Avon and Severn. Fine ancient buildings and many tiny alleys leading off the main street; Baptist Chapel Court leads to one of the oldest Baptist Chapels in England (1655). There are many historic pubs and of course:

Tewkesbury Abbey, completed 1120 and thought to be one of the finest Norman churches in the country. Cathedral-like in its proportions, it has a beautifully decorated central tower, 46ft square and over 130ft high. See also the Abbey Cottages dating from 1450, quite unique and beautifully restored; the museum; Barton Fair *in October* and the Steam Fair and Organ Festival *in July.*

Upton upon Severn
Worcs. Pop 2000. EC Thur. PO, tel, stores, garage. A delightful town, and doubly welcome for being right on the river bank. Interesting timbered and Georgian buildings and 13thC church tower. A good point from which to visit Malvern and the Hills, some six miles to the west. Temporary mooring at the Public Quay or Upton Marina (for a small charge).

Ripple
Worcs. PO, tel, stores. Pretty village with a fine church dating from late 12thC.

Severn Stoke
Worcs. PO, tel, stores. Half timbered pub and church with a curious 14thC side tower.

Hanley Castle
Worcs. Pop 1200. PO, tel, stores. No 13thC castle but a pretty village around a green. Church half 14thC stone, half 17thC brick. Access by lane from the river but mooring is tricky.

Kempsey
Worcs. Pop 1700. PO, tel, stores. A grand church built for the Bishop of Worcester. Some cottages among acres of new housing.

BOATYARDS & BWB

Ⓑ **Sovereign Marine** St Mary's lane, Tewkesbury (292187). On the Mill Avon. R S W D Pump-out (*not Sun*). Boat hire, slipway, gas, mooring.

Ⓑ **Upton Marina** Upton upon Severn, Worcs (Upton 3111) R S W P D Pump-out. Slipway, gas, dry dock, repairs, mooring, chandlery, toilets. Upton Narrowboats and Corsair Cruisers are based here.

BWB Diglis Maintenance Yard Diglis Lock (Worcester 356264)
Ⓑ **Seaborn Yacht Company** Court Meadow, Kempsey, Worcs (Worcester 820295). [R] [S] [W] Pump-out (*not Sat*). Boat hire, slipway, gas, boat building and repairs, mooring, toilets, showers, winter storage. *Closed winter Suns.*

BOAT TRIPS

The 'Avon Belle', a former South Coast boat, runs day trips up and down the Rivers Avon and Severn, starting on the Mill Avon at Tewkesbury. Public service, and private charter trips (maximum 47 passengers). Enquiries to Mrs Rebane, 185 Queens rd, Tewkesbury, Glos. (294088). Small self-drive boats may also be hired from here, by the hour or by the day. Issues BWB River Registration and short term licences. Public slipway nearby. Also weekly cruiser hire.

PUBS

New Bridge Haw Bridge.
Haw Bridge Inn Guess.
Coal House on east bank of river near Apperley. Food.
Yew Tree Inn on west bank of river, opposite Deerhurst. Large pub at the end of a lane. Food.
Plenty of excellent pubs and hotels in Tewkesbury, though none on the River Avon itself.
Lower Lode on the Severn, ¾ of a mile below Tewkesbury Lock. Food. Slipway by the pub, floating moorings. Issues BWB River Registration and short term licences.
Railway Inn Ripple.
Star Hotel Upton. Old free house near the river. Lunches and dinners daily. Residential. (Upton 2300).
Ye Olde Anchor Inn Upton, near the church. This pub is dated 1601.
Three Kings Hanley Castle. Food. B&B. (Upton upon Severn 2686).
Rose & Crown Severn Stoke.

Upton upon Severn. *Derek Pratt.*

River Thames

The Romans called the river 'Isis' from its source to the confluence with the River Thame at Dorchester; below that the names were amalgamated as Thamesis--from that in turn came 'Thames'. The Romans certainly recognised the economic and geographical importance of what is today England's best known river, which runs for 215 miles east to west across the southern counties. Early navigation on the river was a hazardous business, and did not begin to improve until the first pound lock was built at Abingdon in 1630. By the 18thC navigation was surer, and the river was linked to the canal system at several points along its length. Above Teddington the 125 miles of navigable river is admirably controlled by The Thames Conservancy (TWA), with strictly enforced bye-laws and immaculately maintained locks (44 in all), to the benefit of the thousands who use the river each year. For this is no quiet canal--in the summer, especially below Oxford, the river is a thriving holiday centre, crowded with pleasure crafts of every description. Perhaps it is best seen early or late in the year, when its natural beauty can be enjoyed with less distraction.

Navigation on the River Thames

The non-tidal Thames is controlled by the Thames Conservancy Division of the Thames Water Authority. Anyone considering taking a boat on the river should first contact the TC at Nugent House, Vastern Road, Reading, Berks and obtain a copy of the relevant bye-laws.

Those hiring craft will be advised by their hire company of the 'dos and don'ts' of the river, some of the more important being:

No disposal of refuse or sewage into the river.

Keep to the right.

Maximum speed 7 knots, slower if you are creating a disturbance.

Don't cut corners in the river, it may be shallow.

Keep away from weirs.

Moor only at recognised mooring sites.

All locks are attended by resident lock-keepers who work a long, hard day–be courteous and patient at the locks always.

See page 66 for dimensions.

Bampton
Rushey Lock
N
RS Radcot Lock
P
Radcot
Grafton Lock
Eaton Hastings
Kelmscott
W
Buscot Lock
Buscot
P
W St John's Lock
Lechlade
B Limit of navigation
Inglesham

11 miles

Inglesham marks the usual head of navigation for powered craft. Above Oxford the maximum draught is 3ft, headroom 7ft 7ins. On the west side, below Inglesham, the now derelict entrance to the Thames & Severn Canal can be seen, with one of the 'roundhouses', unique to this canal nearby. The river here is isolated and rural. At Rushy Weir there are signs of the former 'flash lock'.

Inglesham
Wilts. A marvellous architectural group around the tiny 13thC church, saved from 19thC 'restoration' by William Morris. Note the bell tower & box pews.

Lechlade
Glos. EC Thur. PO, tel, stores. A golden grey town best viewed from St John's Bridge. Little Farringdon Mill, 1m N, is 18thC and unspoilt.

Buscot
Oxon. Tel, stores. Church with Burne-Jones windows dominated by a beautiful Queen Anne rectory. Nearby is Buscot Park, built 1780 in the Adam style.

Kelmscott
Oxon. PO, tel, stores. Straggling grey stone village. Fine 16thC Manor, home of William Morris 1871-96. 15thC church.

Eaton Hastings
Oxon. PO, store. 13thC church.

Radcot
Oxon. A hamlet. The triple arched bridge is reputedly the oldest on the river. Rowing boats may be hired from the Swan Hotel.
Navigators: steer the northern channel under the single arched bridge.

Bampton
Oxon. PO, tel, stores. An attractive grey stone town with a proliferation of pubs and a fine 13-14thC church. Morris dancing is said to have originated here.

BOATYARDS & SERVICES

Ⓑ **Riverside (Lechlade)** Park end Wharf (Lechlade 52229). W P D Gas, mooring, launching. Hire out launches, punts, canoes, skiffs. *Closed Thur in winter.*

PUBS

Trout Inn Lechlade. Food.
Anchor Inn Eaton Hastings. W
Eagle Bampton. Food, garden.

Oxford

21 miles

The river meanders through pleasant water-meadows and farmland, although the atmosphere changes to that of a canal through the tree lined Shifford Lock Cut. Between Hagley Pool and the Oxford by-pass large colonies of swans are to be seen. Reaching Oxford the navigable river flows through the most unattractive parts of the town, only Christ Church meadows and the Osney Bridge area revealing the 'real' Oxford. The Oxford Canal, heading north, can be joined via Duke's Cut (above Kings Lock) or a more interesting backwater under the north end of Oxford Station. Below Oxford, the draught increases to 4 ft.

Tadpole Bridge
A handsome 18thC arch with a fine old-fashioned pub nearby.

Buckland
Oxon. Intimately connected with Buckland House, one of the most imposing 18thC houses in Berkshire. Church with unusually wide 12thC nave; south transept decorated in rich late Victorian mosaic, c.1890.

Shifford
Oxon. A hamlet and church are all that remain of this once important town.

Standlake
Oxon. PO, tel, stores. An untidy town on the River Windrush.

Hinton Waldrist and Longworth
Oxon. PO, tel, stores. Two pleasant straggling villages on a ridge overlooking the valley. Longworth church has good Arts & Crafts stained glass, 1906.

Newbridge
Oxon. Fine old stone bridge, site of a Civil War battle. The Windrush joins the Thames just above the bridge.

Appleton
Oxon. PO, tel, stores. Meandering stone and thatch village with 12thC Manor and splendid weatherboarded barn and gateway. Some new development to the west.

Cumnor
Oxon. PO, tel, stores. 12thC church with Jacobean and Georgian woodwork. Note the splendid spiral staircase in the tower, dated 1685, and the choir stalls and two-decker pulpit. There is a statue of Queen Elizabeth I in the vestry.

Bablock Hythe
Alas, the ferry, operating for 1000 years, is no more. A Roman stone altar, dredged from the river here, is now in the Ashmolean Museum.

Northmoor
Oxon. PO, tel, stores. 13thC cruxiform church with Tudor rectory.

Stanton Harcourt
Oxon. PO, tel, stores. A superb grey village with a grand cruxiform church. Only Pope's Tower and the Great Kitchen remain of the Harcourts 15thC Manor.

Eynsham
Oxon. EC Wed. MD Thur. PO, tel, stores around the Town Hall in the market square.

Swinford Toll Bridge
Fine stone balustraded bridge and toll house 1777.

Wytham
Oxon. PO, tel, stores. A small village at its best approached from the river. Abbey, 16thC, with many later additions. Visit the marvellous 600 acre Wytham Great Wood.

Godstow
Oxon. The bridge, the Trout Inn and the remains of Godstow Nunnery (destroyed 1646) make a charming setting.

Binsey
Oxon. A tiny hamlet surrounding a green; close by is a Holy Well to St Margaret.

Iffley
Oxon. Norman church with fine west front.

Oxford
Oxon. Pop 109,510. EC Thur, MD Wed. All services. Oxford was founded in the 10thC and has been a university town since the 13thC. Its 39 colleges can be visited, but those noted here have been

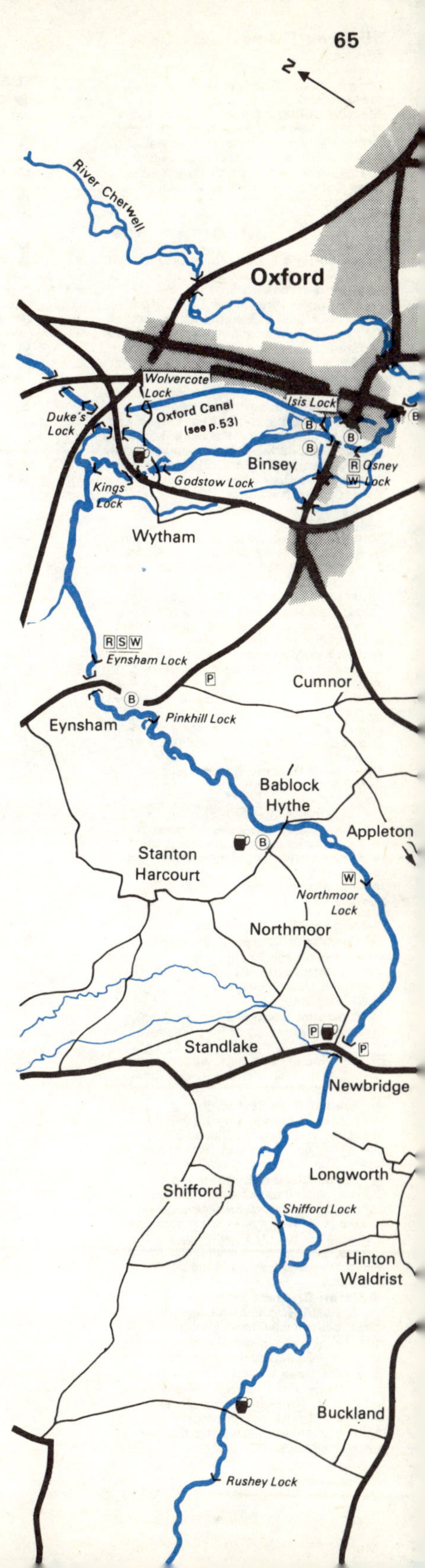

selected as particularly representative of their periods.
Merton College dates from 1264 and is one of the earliest collegiate foundations which are almost unrestored. Typical of the perpendicular and decorative periods. The Grove buildings are by Butterfield.
New College Founded by William of Wykeham, Bishop of Winchester, in 1379. The perpendicular chapel was greatly restored by Sir George Gilbert Scott in the 19thC.
Keble College Built by Butterfield in 1870 entirely in the Victorian Gothic style.
Sheldonian Theatre Broad st. Built by Sir Christopher Wren in the 17thC under the auspices of Gilbert Sheldon, Archbishop of Canterbury, who disapproved of the annual performances of plays which took place in St Mary's. University degrees are awarded here. It has an attractive ceiling by Robert Streeter.
Ashmolean Museum Beaumont st. Outstanding collection of Near Eastern and European archaeology, the Farrer collection of 17thC and 18thC silver, a display of early coins and some drawings of Michelangelo and Raphael. *Open daily.*
Christ Church Gallery Christ Church. Built by Powell and Moya in 1967, and contains drawings by Michelangelo, Veronese and Tintoretto, and 14thC-18thC paintings, mainly Italian. *Open 14.00-16.30. Closed Dec 24-Jan 1 and one week before Easter Sun.*
Museum of Modern Art Pembroke st. Gives unusual art exhibitions–anything from environment to architecture, graphics and photography. *Closed Mon.*
University Museum Parks rd. A high Victorian Gothic building by Deane and Woodward. Natural History, including the head and claw of a Dodo. *Open weekdays.*
Christ Church Meadows Approach from St Aldate's. A path leads down to the Thames, where the rowing eights are to be seen.
University Botanic Garden High st. Oldest botanic garden in Britain, founded by Henry Danvers, Earl of Danby. In the 17thC the garden was intended for the culture of medicinal plants, but today it fosters extensive collections of rare plants for research and teaching. The gateway is by Inigo Jones.
Information Bureau St Aldate's. (Oxford 48707).

BOATYARDS & SERVICES

Ⓑ **Caribbean Cruisers** Eynsham. ¼ mile downstream from Pinkhill Lock, on the east bank. (Oxford 881698). R S W P D Pump-out. Gas, slipway, cruiser hire. *Closed winter weekends.*

Ⓑ **Bossoms Boatyard** Oxford, Medley. Opposite southern tip of Port Meadow, on west bank. (Oxford 47780). Chandlery, 27 foot slipway, moorings, winter storage, boat sales and repairs, motor sales, fibre-glass boatbuilding.

Ⓑ **Medley Boat Station** Oxford. (511660). On the southern tip of Port Meadow, on east bank. Cruiser hire. R S D Pump-out. Boat and motor repairs. Gas, mooring, chandlery, toilets.

Ⓑ **Osney Marine Engineering** Oxford. In small backwater to the east of Osney Lock (entrance to backwater is 150 yards upstream of lock, on east side). (Oxford 41348). R S W P D 30ft slipway, gas, moorings, winter storage, boat and motor repairs, toilets. Club and bar facilities.

Ⓑ **Safari Cruisers** Littlemore. Heyford Hill Boatyard. ¾ mile downstream from Iffley Lock, on east bank. (Oxford 777371). R S W D Pump-out. Cruiser hire. Gas, boat crane. *Closed winter weekends.*

Ⓑ **Salter Bros** Oxford. Immediately downstream of Folly Bridge, on west bank. (43421/2). W P D Pump-out. Hire cruisers and day boats. Chandlery, gas, boat building and repair, provisions. *Closed winter weekends.*

PUBS & RESTAUANTS

The Trout Inn Tadpole Bridge. Collection of stuffed fish, all caught locally. Food, camping, fishing.
✕ **Rose Revived Inn** Newbridge. Fishing.
Harcourt Arms Stanton Harcourt. Food.
Plough Appleton. Food.
✕ **The Trout Inn** Godstow. Dates from 12thC, peacocks in the garden.
Talbot Eynsham. Food.
Turf Green Hidden away down St Helen's Passage, New College Lane, Oxford. Good beer and cheese; mulled wine in winter.
Watermans Arms South Street, Osney.
Tree Hotel Iffley. Food, garden.
. . . and many more fine pubs in Oxford.
There are several very good restaurants in Oxford. Here are three of them.
✕ **Restaurant Elizabeth** 84 St Aldate's Oxford. (42230). Easily the best restaurant in town. Superb Basque food and a remarkable wine list. *Open dinners and Sun lunch. Closed most of Aug.*
✕ **La Sorbonne** 130A High Street, Oxford. (41320). Smart French restaurant –frog's legs and all–in a 17thC building. *Lunch & dinner Mon-Sat. Closed for 2 weeks at end of Aug.*
✕ **Lotus House** 197 Banbury Road, Oxford. (54239). Prawns with chilli sauce, spare ribs, toffee apples. *Open 12.00-14.30, 18.00-23.45.*

River Thames Dimensions

Lock sizes are: Teddington to Reading 132ft · 17ft 6 ins. Reading to Oxford 120ft · 17ft 3 ins. Oxford to Inglesham 109ft · 14ft. Craft of more than 7ft 7 ins above the waterline cannot navigate beyond Oxford.

For information on hire craft on the river, write to The Thames Hire Cruiser Association, c/o Godalming Narrow Boats, Farncombe Boat House, Godalming.

Abingdon

24 miles

The river is tree lined leaving Oxford, affording only glimpses of the flat surroundings. Passing to the east of Abingdon, the river is dominated by the gaol, then two 'lock cuts' straighten the course before it sweeps in a wide arc to Dorchester. By Wallingford is the stretch featured in Jerome K. Jerome's 'Three Men in a Boat'.

Radley
Oxon. PO, tel, stores. A commuter town. Church with 15thC pulpit canopy, reputedly from the House of Commons. Radley College famed as a rowing school.
Nuneham Courtenay
Oxon. 18thC model village with splendidly situated mansion in wooded grounds to the water's edge.
Abingdon
Oxon. EC Thur. MD Mon. PO, tel, stores. An attractive 18thC market town. The gaol, 1805-11, is an impressive stone bastille. Perpendicular style church with five aisles. Fine Town hall by Kempster, one of Wren's city masons.
Culham
Oxon. PO, stores. 17thC Culham Manor overlooks Culham Cut. Good walks here.
Sutton Courtenay
Oxon. PO, tel, stores. Large village built around a green. The church has late Norman work and a Jacobean pulpit. Eric Blair (George Orwell) is buried here. Late 12thC manor and 14thC Abbey, now used as a school.
Long Wittenham
Oxen. PO, stores. A fine straggling village with 13thC church. Museum.
Clifton Hampden
Oxon. PO, tel, stores. An excellent situation, dominated by the bridge, 1864. The church overlooks the river.
Dorchester
Oxon. EC Wed. PO, tel, stores. One of the oldest English cities. The abbey has a fine Jesse window, its stonework imitating trees, and a lifelike effigy of Sir John Holcombe. The Old Monastery Guest House is a museum.
Warborough
Oxon. PO, stores. A traditional English village around a green.
Shillingford
Oxon. Well situated triple arched bridge.
Ewelme
Oxon. PO, stores. A picture book brick and flint village not to be missed. A 15thC survival among the watercress beds. Three miles from the river.
Wallingford
Oxon. EC Wed. MD Fri. PO, tel, stores. One of the oldest Royal boroughs receiving its charter in 1155. St Peter's Church, 1777, has an unusual openwork spire. Town Hall 1670. Fine bridge of medieval origin with 17 arches.
Navigators: use the centre arch.

BOATYARDS & SERVICES

Ⓑ **Abingdon Boat Centre** Abingdon (21125) W P D Pump-out. Cruiser hire, gas, chandlery, slipway. *Closed winter Suns.*
Ⓑ **Red Line Cruisers** Abingdon (21562) W P D Pump-out, cruiser hire. *Closed winter Suns.*
Ⓑ **Wallingford Bridge Boathouse** Wallingford (38005). Chandlery, mooring, slipway, repairs, boat & engine sales. Toilets, gas. Day boat hire.
Ⓑ **Maidboats** Wallingford (36163). R S W P D Cruiser hire, gas, slipway, pump-out, toilets, repairs. *Closed winter Suns.*

PUBS

- **Fox** Sandford.
- **Old Anchor** Abingdon. Riverside.
- **Waggon & Horses** Culham. Food.
- **Plough** Clifton Hampden. Food.
- ✕ **Barley Mow** Clifton Hampden.
- **Chequers** Dorchester.
- **Castle** Benson. Food.
- **Coachmakers Arms** Wallingford.

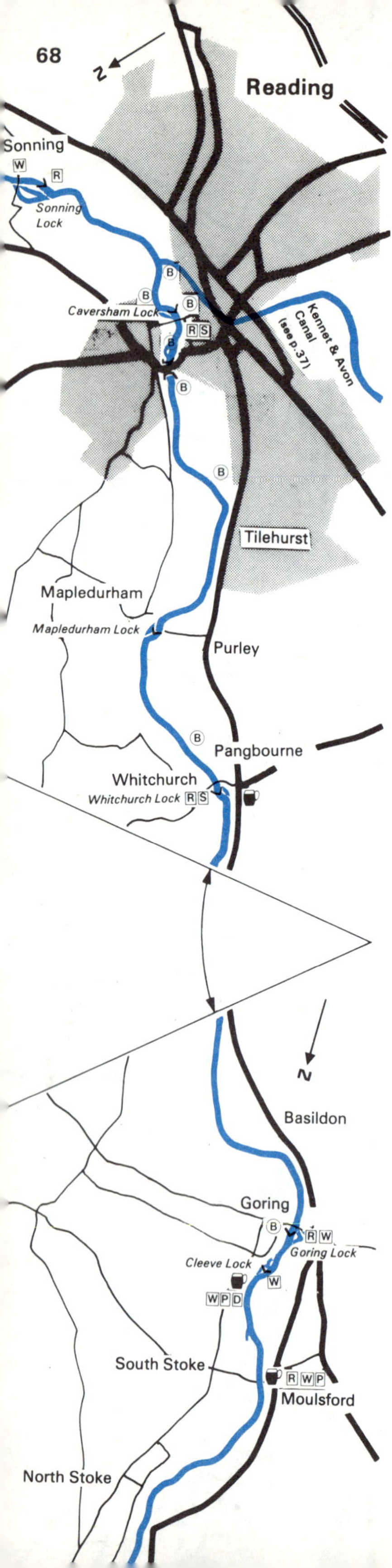

Reading

17 miles

Passing the reputedly haunted islands by Moulsford railway bridge, the river approaches the stretch between Goring and Mapledurham, one of its most attractive parts. Beech woods rise steeply on the east bank above Pangbourne while opposite there are extensive meadows. However this soon gives way to suburbia and industry nearer Reading. The draught from here to Windsor increases to 4ft 6ins.

North Stoke
Oxon. PO, stores. An attractive red brick village set among trees. Pleasingly original church.

South Stoke
Oxon. Residential village hidden by trees.

Moulsford
Oxon. PO, stores. A roadside village. Small secluded church rebuilt by Gilbert Scott 1846. Moulsford Rail Bridge; four beautiful brick arches by Brunel.

Goring
Oxon. EC Wed. PO, tel, stores. With Streatly, set in a splendid, deep wooded valley, by one of the most spectacular reaches on the river. The church has one of the oldest bells in England, 1290. Excellent walks on Goring Heath.

Basildon
Berks. An attractive architectural group, with an over restored 13thC church. Basildon Park is a splendid Georgian mansion built by John Carr in 1776 (private).

Pangbourne
Berks. EC Thur. PO, tel, stores. A large commuter town still preserving a trace of Edwardian elegance. Nautical College, an imposing William and Mary style mansion, by Sir John Belcher 1897-8.

Whitchurch
Berks. Good mill buildings overlooked by the church. Toll bridge.

Hardwick House
Oxon. Between Whitechurch and Mapledurham. Mainly Tudor house with gardens almost down to the river (private).

Purley
Berks. Straggling village. Church by Street 1870, with 17thC brick tower. Purley Park, 1800, is a fine white Portland stone house overlooking the river. 17thC Purley Hall stands in attractive grounds, but is private; its pretty late Georgian entrance lodges can be admired from the road.

Tilehurst
Berks. Sprawling Reading suburb. Church of St Michael, Street 1856, has an exquisite William Morris east window, depicting angels around the Virgin and child.

Mapledurham
One of the oldest corn and grist mills on the Thames, some cottages, Mapledurham House and a church. Typical of a late 19thC landscape painting. The house was the setting for the closing chapters of the 'Forsythe Saga'.

Reading
Berks. All services. A mixture of university and industry, the town lacks a cohesive centre, but has plenty of interest. Fragmentary remains of the 12thC abbey lie on the edge of Forbury Park. The Gaol, Scott and Moffat 1842-4, is an imposing castellated keep. The Royal Berkshire Hospital, 1837-9, has a magnificient Bath stone façade. Reading Museum & Art Gallery, Friar st, has one of the most interesting archaeological collections in the country. Caversham is a continuation of Reading, on the north bank.

BOATYARDS & SERVICES

Ⓑ **Hobbs** Goring (2106). Day hire launches, mooring.

Ⓑ **Reading Marine Services** Reading (27155). W P D Gas, mooring, slipway, chandlery.

Ⓑ **Bridge Boats** Reading (50346) R S W D Pump-out, cruiser hire, gas, slipway, repairs, toilets, showers. *Closed winter Suns.*

Ⓑ **Kennet Mouth Boathouse** Reading (64186). [W] Small craft hire, gas, chandlery, repairs.
Ⓑ **Reading Marine** Crane Wharf, Reading (53917) [R][S][W][D] Pump-out. Hire cruisers, mooring. 1m up River Kennet.
Ⓑ **Salter Bros** Reading (Oxford 43421) [W][D] Pump-out. Hire craft, river trips. *Closed winter weekends.*
Ⓑ **Caversham Marina** Reading (53917) [W][D] Pump-out (*not Sun*). Boat hire, slipway, gas, dry dock, boat building and repairs, mooring, storage. *Closed winter weekends.*
Ⓑ **Better Boating Co** Mill Green, Caversham, Reading (479536) [R][S][W][D] Pump-out. Gas, toilets, provisions, storage, crane.

PUBS & RESTAURANTS

George Hotel Wallingford. Tudor.
Perch & Pike South Stoke
Olde Leatherne Bottel Goring. Fine old riverside inn.
Miller of Mansfield Goring. 18thC.
Greyhound Whitchurch. Village pub.
Swan Hotel Pangbourne. Food, riverside.
Clifton Arms Cavenham. Food.
George Hotel Reading. 16thC inn.

Marlow

17 miles

After the chilly atmosphere of Reading, the river through Sonning is lined with willows through which hotels and smart houses can be seen. At Marsh, ivy covered cliffs capped with beech woods rise on the east bank. The wooden boat houses on this reach are superb. Reaching Henley, famous for its Regatta, the river is particularly attractive and popular, with a good mill at Hambledon.

Sonning
Berks. EC Tue. MD Sat. PO, stores. A picture book Thames-side village, with an eleven arched 18thC brick bridge and a 19thC church, remarkable for its monuments. South of the town is the spectacular 60ft deep Sonning Railway Cutting, engineered by Brunel in 1839.

Shiplake
Oxon. PO, stores. A high class commuter village with a well situated church, containing old Belgian glass of great beauty.

Wargrave
Berks. EC Wed. PO, stores. A largely Georgian cruciform town, well situated among trees. The original church was burnt down in 1914 by the Suffragettes–its replacement is

Marlow, River Thames. *Derek Pratt.*

Marlow (cont)

pleasing. By the river is the 19thC Wargrave Manor.

Harpsden
Oxon. An attractive village, with a tidy church. In the farm opposite the church the barns are walled with wooden wall-paper and fabric printing blocks, a most unusual and decorative effect.

Henley
Oxon. EC Wed. MD Thur. All services. A fine market town, with an 18thC stone bridge. The main street has a feeling of timelessness and Edwardian elegance. A popular place in summer.

Temple Island
The Temple was built as a vista for the nearby Fawley Court, 1684.

Medmenham
Bucks. PO, stores. A village straggling up from the Thames into the woods behind. The orgiastic 'Hell Fire Club' under the auspices of Sir Francis Dashwood, no longer resides in the Abbey.

Hambledon
Bucks. PO, stores. A 14thC church and a 17thC manor in a fine village setting round a green, all mellow brick and flint. Notable weatherboarded mill by the lock.

Harleyford Manor
Built in 1755 by Sir Robert Taylor. Splendid grounds, reputedly by Capability Brown.

Bisham
Bucks. PO, store. Largely Georgian, with a church and an abbey bordering the river. Partly Norman church.

Marlow
Bucks. EC Wed. MD Mon. All services. A fine Georgian town. The suspension bridge built by Tierny Clarke in 1831-6, and restored in 1966, has a good view of the weir.

BOATYARDS & SERVICES

Ⓑ **John Bushnell** Wargrave (2161). [R][S][W][P][D] Pump-out. Slipway, gas, repairs. Boat hire.

Ⓑ **Swancraft** Wargrave (2577). [R][W] Pump-out. Hire craft, boat building, launching.

Ⓑ **Val Wyatt Marine** Wargrave (3211). [W][P][D] Chandlery, gas, slipway, sales, repairs.

Ⓑ **Hobbs & Sons** Henley (2035). [R][W][P][D] Cruiser hire, chandlery, slipway, sales, repairs, moorings, storage.

Ⓑ **A. Parrott** Henley (2380). Launch hire, gas, chandlery, moorings, repairs.

Ⓑ **Peter Freebody** Hurley (Littlewick Green 4382). [R][W] Gas, chandlery, slipway, moorings, sales and repairs.

Ⓑ **Harleyford Marina** Marlow (71361). [R][S][W] Extensive moorings, gas, chandlery, launching, sales and repairs. Toilets, showers, provisions.

Ⓑ **J. G. Meakes** Marlow (6911). [W][P][D] Gas, chandlery, slipway, moorings, repairs.

Ⓑ **Bourne End Marina** Bourne End (22813). [W][D] Moorings, chandlery. Gas, toilets, provisions.

Ⓑ **Wootens** Cookham Dean (Marlow 4244). [R][S][W] Slipway, mooring, boat building, gas, toilets.

Ⓑ **Andrews' Boathouse** Bourne End (22314). [R][S][W][P][D] Pump-out, cruiser hire, mooring, gas, chandlery, sales, repairs, lavatories, showers.

PUBS & RESTAURANTS

Bull Sonning. Food lunchtime.

Plowden Arms Shiplake.

✕ **St George & Dragon** Wargrave riverside. Note the old hotel sign in the bar.

Bull Wargrave. Food.

Angel on the Bridge Henley riverside. Food. Large garden.

✕ **Little White Hart** Henley riverside.

Red Cross Henley. Opposite the brewery.

Dog & Badger Medmenham. 14thC.

✕ **Burgers** The Causeway, Marlow. Continental confectioners. *Closes 18.00, Mon aft, Sun.*

Clayton Arms Marlow.

✕ **Complete Angler** Marlow Bridge. Good view of weir, continental cooking.

Ship Marlow. Food.

Spade Oak Bourne End.

Windsor

14 miles

Between Cookham and Maidenhead wooded banks rise almost vertically on the east side. This is followed by a pleasant but unremarkable stretch before Windsor Castle and Eton College are sighted. After Windsor, the river is flanked by houses and bungalows. Draught from Windsor to Staines 5ft 6 ins

Bourne End
Bucks. EC Wed. PO, stores. A riverside commuter town and sailing centre.

Cookham
Berks. EC Thur. PO, stores. An attractive, well preserved village, home of Stanley Spencer. The iron bridge overlooks the partly 12thC church.

Cliveden
Fine house built by Barry in 1862 for the Astor family, concealed by beechwoods. Excellent tapestries and furniture. Now a N.T. property.

Maidenhead
Berks. EC Thur. MD Fri/Sat. All services. A dormitory suburb of London, at its best from the river. Notable balustraded bridge by Sir Robert Taylor 1772-7. The rail bridge, Brunel 1839, has the largest brick spans in the world, 123ft.

Bray
Berks. PO, stores. Commuter town retaining its village centre. 13thC church with a fine brick gatehouse, 1450. Ockwells Manor, an elegant and refined timber framed house, stands 1 mile SW of Bray.

Dorney
Berks. PO, stores. Dorney Court and church, forming a perfect unit, survive in suburbia.

Boveney
Berks. A village around a green, with a secluded riverside church.

Windsor
Berks. EC Wed. MD Thur. All services A largely Victorian town owing its existence to the fairy tale castle, one of the grandest in England, built 1165-79 by Henry II, with additions and alterations by succeeding monarchs. A must to visit, *open 10.00-dusk.* Windsor Great Park covers 4,800 acres and is *open daily.* Town Hall by Wren, 1689-90.

Eton
Berks. EC Wed. PO, stores. Famed for its College, founded 1440 by Henry VI. Chapel, cloisters and playing fields are *open daily.* The long and rambling High Street makes a pleasant walk.

Old Windsor
PO, stores. The old village exists by the river built around the site of a Saxon Royal Palace. 13thC church restored by Gilbert Scott 1863.

Ankerwyke Priory
A 19thC mansion, surrounded by yew trees, one 33ft round the trunk.

Runnymede
Surrey. A stretch of parkland famed for its memorials to Magna Carta and Kennedy. Many good walks.

Staines
Middx. EC Thur. MD Wed/Sat. A commuter town, still pleasant around the church. Clarence Street, which culminates in Rennie's stone bridge, built 1829-32, still has the feeling of an 18thC market town.

Laleham
Surrey. PO, stores. The well situated church contains the grave of Matthew Arnold.

Chertsey
Surrey. EC Wed. MD Sat. All services. A town with some 18thC feeling, especially around Windsor Street.

BOATYARDS & SERVICES

These are in abundance hereabouts, so only essential information is given.

Ⓑ **Bert Bushnell** Maidenhead (24061) R S W P D Pump-out.

Ⓑ **Bourne End Marina** Bourne End (22813). R S W P D

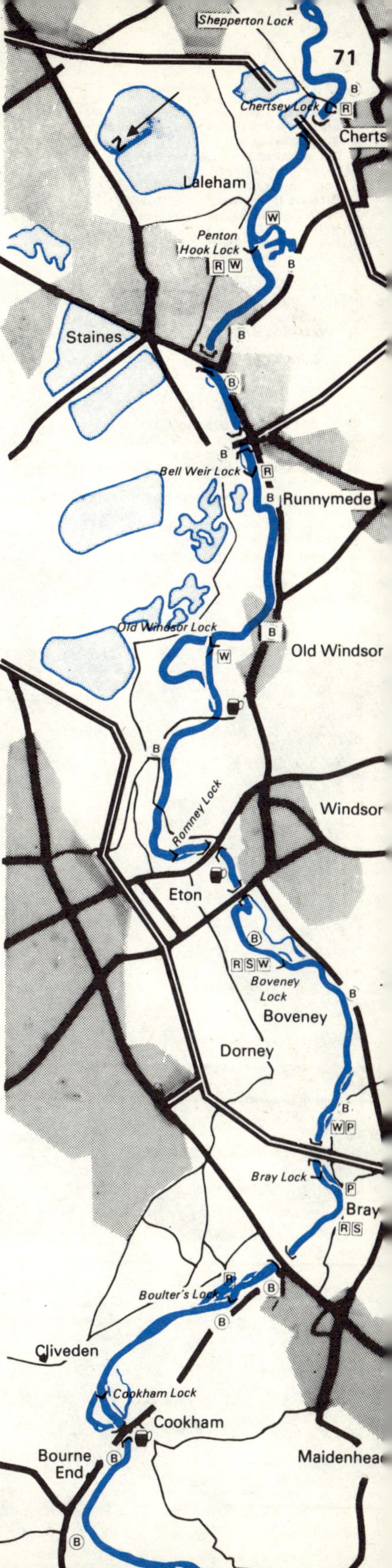

Ⓑ **Turk & Sons** Bourne End (20110). [W]
Ⓑ **Andrews Bros** Maidehead (24056). [W]
Ⓑ **Bray Marina** Bray (23654). [R][W][P][D]
Ⓑ **Racecourse Yacht Basin** Windsor (51501). [R][S][W][P][D]
Ⓑ **Tom Jones** Windsor (60699). [W]
Ⓑ **Biffens Boatyard** Staines (52408). [D]
Ⓑ **John Hicks** Datchet (Slough 43930). [S][W][D] Pump-out.
Ⓑ **Penton Hook Marina** Chertsey (01-892 2861). [W][D] Access from Chertsey side only.
Ⓑ **Crevalds** Windsor (60393). [R][S][W][P][D] Gas, mooring, toilets.
Ⓑ **J Tims** Staines (52093). [R][S][W][D]
Ⓑ **Waterline Holidays** Next to Staines railway bridge (Staines 61401). [R][S][W][D] Gas, toilets, mooring.

PUBS & RESTAURANTS

Bel and the Dragon Cookham.
Vine Market street, Maidenhead.
Crown Bray. Village local.
Waterside Inn Bray. Restaurant with riverside terrace.
Watermans Arms Eton. Next to the boathouse.
There are many good pubs in Windsor.
Lord Nelson Old Windsor.
Great Fosters Egham. Hotel and restaurant in a 16thC moated house.
Turks Head Laleham.
George Chertsey.

Hampton Court

14 miles

The Thames rubs shoulders with the stock-brokers at Weybridge, where the River Wey joins. The pleasant clutter of Hampton follows, with the park to the west, and light industry and housing to the east. Draught from Staines to Teddington 6ft 6ins.

Weybridge
Surrey. EC Wed. All services. The junction of the Thames and Wey is marked by a pretty iron bridge of 1865.
Shepperton
Middx. PO, stores. Still surviving as a village, with some intact 18thC inns. The 17-18thC church has box pews; the rectory to the north has an excellent Queen Anne front.
Walton-on-Thames
Surrey. EC Wed. A shopping centre.
Sunbury
Middx. PO, stores. Has a village feeling.
East Molesey
Surrey. Good riverside facing Hampton.
Hampton
Middx. PO, stores. An attractive late 18thC village, whose church dominates the river. Also by the river is Garrick's Temple. Visit a real Swiss chalet, brought over in 1899.

Hampton Court, River Thames. *Derek Pratt.*

Hampton Court (cont)

Hampton Court
Probably the greatest secular building in England. Built by Cardinal Wolsey in 1514 and taken over by Henry VIII in 1529. Now occupied by Royal Pensioners. Gardens contain the Maze and Great Vine, planted 1769. *Open daily.*

Hampton Green
Some fine buildings around a green.

Thames Ditton
Surrey. PO, stores. A village centre unspoilt except for the din of Heathrow's jets.

Surbiton
Surrey. PO, stores. Suburbiton.

Kingston
Surrey. EC Wed. MD Mon/Sat. All services. A Royal Borough where seven Saxon kings were crowned. Good river frontage around the stone bridge. Pretty market place with an Italianate Town Hall, hounded by traffic.

Teddington
Middx. PO, stores. The weir is the largest on the river, marking the boundary between tidal and non-tidal Thames.

Ham
Surrey, PO, stores. Built around a common, with Ham House, a superb 17thC riverside mansion, the centre of attraction. Some good 20thC development.

Twickenham
Middx. All services. Elegant and desirable in the 18thC, now suburbia. Strawberry Hill House remains one of the most important Gothic revival buildings still standing.

BOATYARDS & SERVICES

These are in abundance hereabouts, so only essential information is given.

Ⓑ **W Bates & Son** Chertsey (62255). R S W P D Pump-out.

Ⓑ **Chertsey Meads Marine** Downstream of Chertsey Bridge (Chertsey 64699). R S W D

Ⓑ **G R Dunton** Walton (21878). W

Ⓑ **Starley Marine** Walton (24407) W

Ⓑ **D B H Marine** Walton (28019). W D

Ⓑ **Weybridge Marine** Weybridge (47453). R S W D Pump-out.

Ⓑ **T W Allen & Son** East Molesey (01-979 1997). R S W D Pump-out.

Ⓑ **Turks of Sunbury** Sunbury (82028). R W D

Ⓑ **G Wilson** Sunbury (82067). W

Ⓑ **Hucks** Hampton (01-979 2135). W D

Ⓑ **Ambrose Sillette & Brian Ambrose** Hampton (01-979 3447). W P D

Ⓑ **Maidboats** Thames Ditton (01-398 0271). R S W D Pump-out.

Ⓑ **Thames Ditton Marina** Thames Ditton (01-398 6159). R S W P D

Ⓑ **R J Turk & Sons** Kingston (01-546 2434). R W Pump-out.

Ⓑ **The Tough Brothers** Teddington (01-977 4494). W D

PUBS & RESTAURANTS

✕🍷 **Casa Romana** Temple Hall, Weybridge. Italian cooking.

🍺 **Old Crown** Weybridge. Timbered pub.

🍺 **Swan** Walton-on-Thames.

🍺 **White Hart** Hampton.

🍺 **Albion** East Molesey. Food lunchtime.

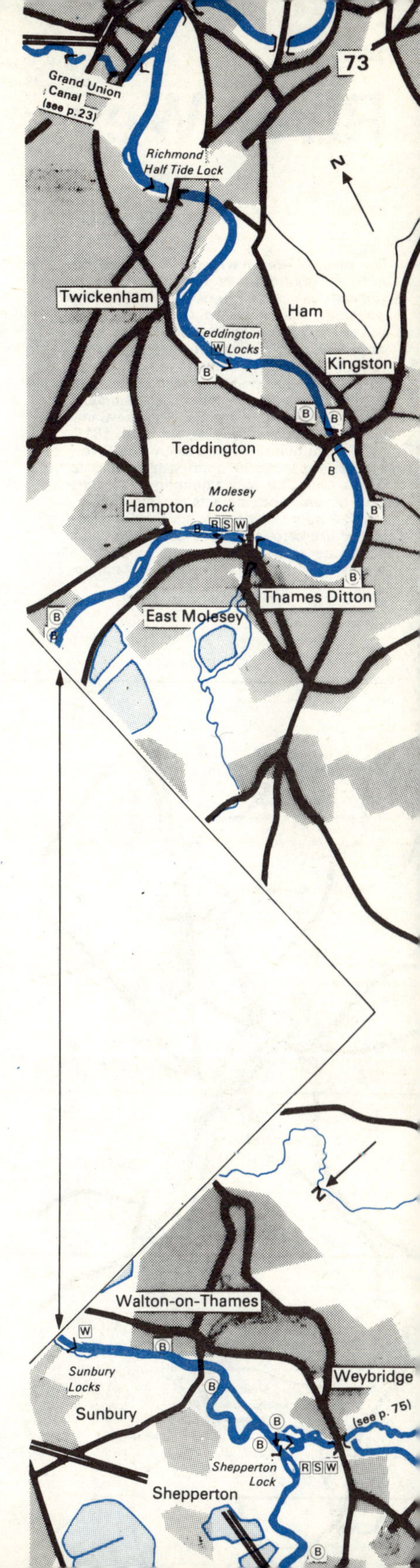

River Wey

The present Wey navigation to Guildford, with its pound locks and ten miles of artificial cut, was opened in 1653. The remaining four miles to Godalming were opened in 1760. Considerable barge traffic was soon using the route. It carried agricultural produce, timber and Farnham Pottery ware to London, and manufactured goods and grain in the other direction. With the building of the Basingstoke Canal in 1796 and the Wey & Arun in 1816, trade continued to thrive on the Wey, and as late as 1969 grain was carried to Coxes Mill. The two adjoining canals are now closed, and there is no more commercial traffic, pleasure craft having replaced the barges. Owned by the National Trust, the river is now quite popular, a surprisingly rural waterway close to London.

Navigation on the River Wey

All craft using the river must be registered and licensed with the National Trust, and are subject to their bye-laws.
Navigation Office:
Dapdune Lea, Wharf Road, Guildford, Surrey. (Guildford 61389).
Boats with a draught of over 2ft 6ins MUST consult the lock keeper at Thames Lock BEFORE entering from the Thames. Temporary lock passes can be bought here, and a 1in spigot windlass can be obtained.
Maximum draught: Weybridge to Guildford 3ft 3ins; Guildford to Godalming 2ft 6ins.
Maximum headroom: Weybridge to Guildford 7ft; Guildford to Godalming 6ft.
All locks are 73ft 6ins × 13ft 10ins.
Speed limit: 4 knots.

9 miles

The head of navigation, near the heavy stone bridge, seems isolated from Godalming. Leaving the town, the hills and trees of the North Downs close in, before the navigation passes through the centre of Guildford. The Yvonne Arnaud theatre is sited on the lock island, and there are interesting mill and wharf buildings.

Godalming
Surrey. EC Wed. PO, tel, stores. The limit of navigation. By tradition a cloth making town, its confusion of streets have plenty to offer, including a pretty 19thC Market Hall, and a church with a 13thC lead spire.

Shalford
Surrey. EC Wed. PO, tel, stores. Rustic in parts, but at its best near the river. Just south of the town is the junction with the old Wey & Arun Canal—alas only the first 100yds are still in water.

Guildford
Surrey. EC Wed. All services. A compact town and cultural centre built on the steep sides of the Wey valley. The High Street is attractive, with good buildings of all periods. The modern architecture of the University of Surrey is better than most. Guildford Cathedral is an unsubtle Gothic revival building started in 1932 and completed in 1966—more satisfactory inside than out.

BOATYARDS & SERVICES

Ⓑ **Godalming Narrow Boats** Godalming (21306). R S W D Pump-out. Narrow boat hire, boat builders, Rowing boat and canoe hire. River trips. Gas, mooring, chandlery, toilets, provisions.

Ⓑ **Leroy's Boathouse** Guildford (504494). R S W D Pump-out. Hire narrow and wide beam boats. Small boat hire, trip boats to Guildford. Gas, dry dock, toilets.

Guildford Waterside Centre Guildford (72881). R S W Water recreation centre.

Ⓑ **Plancraft Marine** Guildford (62213). Boatbuilders and chandlers.

PUBS

- **King's Arms Royal** Godalming
- **Star** Godalming.
- **Sea Horse** Shalford. Food, garden.
- **Jolly Farmer** Guildford riverside.
- **Row Barge** Guildford riverside. Garden.

Weybridge

10 miles

After Guildford the navigation ambles through a mixture of countryside and suburbs, fortunately just keeping the latter at a distance. The river joins the Thames at Weybridge. Its architecture, lock and mill buildings, provide some highlights en route.

Send
Surrey. EC Wed. PO, tel, stores. Attractively placed church and 18thC houses that look good from the river.

Newark Priory
Surrey. An enticing and romantic ruin of a 12thC flint priory. There is no right of way up the backwaters that pass its broken walls.

Pyrford
Surrey. EC Wed. Stores. A rare real village among watermeadows and trees. Almost intact Norman church and many houses of interest.

The Basingstoke Canal
Opened in 1794, only the initial $\frac{1}{4}$ mile is now navigable. Houseboats fill the first few lock pounds, isolated by the broken locks. Much of the canal is still in water, and the course, up to the collapsed Greywell Tunnel, is intact. An enthusiastic group of supporters are working to re-open the navigation – some sections are now navigable, and it is hoped through navigation will be restored in the 1980's. Meanwhile, the towpath makes an excellent walk.

Byfleet
Surrey. EC Wed. PO, tel, stores. The 13thC church and 17thC brick manor house can be found in the midst of much commuter housing. North of here was the old Brooklands Racetrack, with its legendary bankings, now an aircraft factory.

Coxes Mill
Surrey. A superb group of 19thC mill buildings overlook Coxes Lock. The mill is still in use – sadly the grain no longer comes by barge.

Weybridge
Surrey. EC Wed. All services. Much 'stockbroker' Tudor – the western edge of London's suburban sprawl.

PUBS

- **New Inn** Send. Riverside, garden.
- **Ship** Ripley.
- **Anchor** Pyrford Lock. Riverside, garden.
- **White Hart** New Haw Lock. Riverside, garden.
- **Pelican** Coxes Lock. Riverside, garden.
- **Old Crown** Weybridge. Timbered pub.

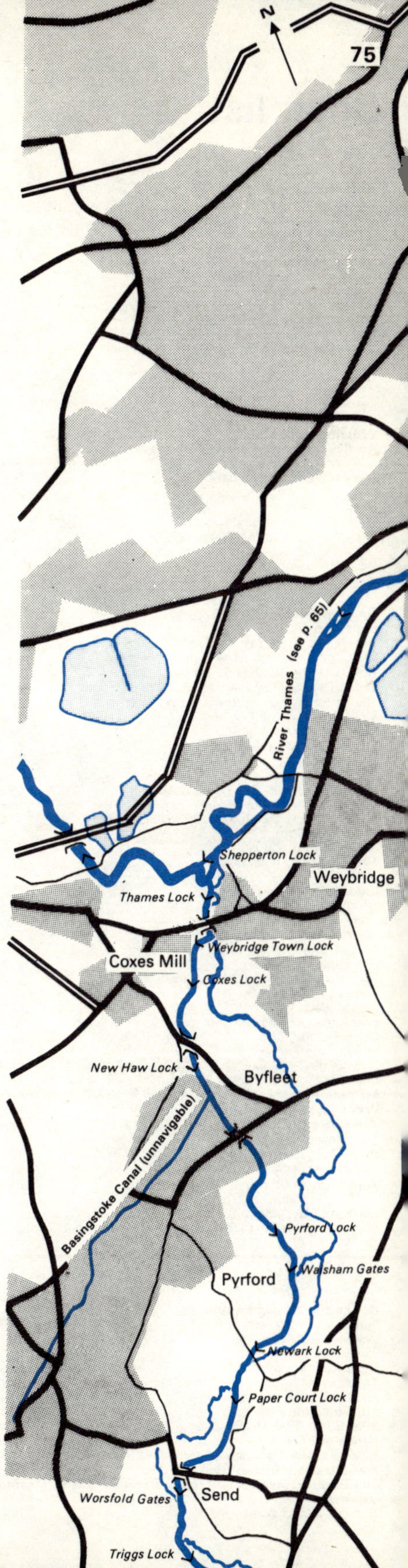

Book list

Reference works:

Title	Author	Publisher
Canals and Rivers of Britain	Andrew Darwin	Dent
Shell Book of Inland Waterways	Hugh McKnight	David & Charles
Canal Architecture in Britain	Frances Pratt	B.W.B.
Inland Waterways of Great Britain and Northern Ireland	L. A. Edwards	Imray
A General History of Inland Navigation (reprint from 1805)	J. Phillips	David & Charles
Historical Account of Navigable Rivers & Canals of Great Britain (reprint from 1831)	J. Priestley	David & Charles
Bradshaw's Canals & Navigable rivers of England and Wales (reprint from 1904)	Henry de Salis	David & Charles

Cruising books:

Title	Author	Publisher
Holiday Cruising on Inland Waterways	Charles Hadfield & Michael Streat	David & Charles
The Canals Book (annual)		Link House Publications
Canal Cruising	John Hankinson	Ward Lock
Waterway Users Companion		BWB Annual
Real Ale Guide to the Waterways	Alan Hill	Nicholson/CAMRA

General books:

Title	Author	Publisher
British Canals	Charles Hadfield	David & Charles
The Canals of the East Midlands	Charles Hadfield	David & Charles
The Canals of the West Midlands	Charles Hadfield	David & Charles
The Canals of South & South East England	Charles Hadfield	David & Charles
James Brindley Engineer, 1716–1772	C. T. G. Boucher	Goose & Son
The Decorative arts of the mariner	G. F. Cook (ed.)	Cassell's
Slow Boat through England	Frederic Doerflinger	Allan Wingate
Canals in Camera	John Gagg	Ian Allan
English Canals (in 3 volumes)	D. D. Gladwin & J. M. White	Oakwood Press
The Canal Age	Charles Hadfield	David & Charles; and Pan Books
The Canal Enthusiast's Handbook	Charles Hadfield (ed.)	David & Charles
Canals and their Architecture	Robert Harris	Hugh Evelyn
A tour of the Grand Junction Canal in 1819 (reprinted 1968)	J. Hassell	Cranfield & Bonfiel
Journeys of the Swan	John Liley	Allen & Unwin
The Canals of England	Eric de Maré	The Architectural Press
Canal & River Craft in pictures	Hugh McKnight	David & Charles
Discovering Canals	Leon Metcalfe & John Vince	Shire Publications
Water Highways	David Owen	Phoenix House
Water Rallies	David Owen	Phoenix House
Narrow Boat	L. T. C. Rolt	Eyre & Spottiswoode
Navigable Waterways	L. T. C. Rolt	Longmans
The Inland Waterways of England	L. T. C. Rolt	Allen & Unwin
Thomas Telford	L. T. C. Rolt	Longmans
James Watt	L. T. C. Rolt	Batsford
Lost Canals of England and Wales	R. Russell	David & Charles
Canal Fishing	Kenneth Seaman	Barrie & Jackson
Voyage into England	John Seymour	David & Charles
Lives of the Engineers (in 3 volumes—reprint from 1862)	Samuel Smiles	David & Charles
Maidens Trip	Emma Smith	Penguin
Waterways Heritage	P. Smith	Luton Museum
The Flower of Gloster (reprint from 1911)	Temple Thurston	David & Charles
Hold on a Minute	T. Wilkinson	Allen & Unwin
River Navigation in England 1600–1750	T. S. Willan	F. Cass
The Kennet & Avon Canal	Kenneth R. Clew	David & Charles
Waterways to Stratford	Charles Hadfield & John Norris	David & Charles
London's lost route to Basingstoke	P. A. L. Vine	David & Charles
London's lost route to the Sea	P. A. L. Vine	David & Charles

Books for Young People

Title	Author	Publisher
Fun on the Waterways	J. Banks & P. Hume	Penwork
Waterways Atlas of the British Isles	John Cranfield & Michael Bonfiel	Cranfield & Bonfiel
Canals of the World	Charles Hadfield	Basil Blackwell
The Cow who fell in the Canal (Drawings coloured and to colour)	Phyllis Krasilovsky	Penguin
Curlew on the Cut	Beatrice Lawrence	Geoffrey Dibb
Your Book of Waterways	Eric de Maré	Faber
Canals in Britain	Alison Ross	Basil Blackwell
River & Canal Transport (Approaches to Environmental Studies Book 7)	John Vince	Blandford
The Transport Revolution (Focus on History Series paperback)	Roger Watson	Longmans
Britain's Inland Waterways	Roger Wickson	Methuen

Specialist publications:

Title	Author	Publisher
The Facts about the Waterways	British Waterways Board	HMSO 1965
Leisure and the Waterways	British Waterways Board	HMSO 1967
British Waterways Board Annual Report	British Waterways Board	HMSO
London's Canal	Herbert Spencer	Putnam 1961
The Colne Valley: Studies for a Regional Park	Colne Valley Working Party	Bucks. County Council 1967
A Lee Valley Regional Park	Civic Trust	Civic Trust 1964
The Lee Valley Regional Park		L.V.R.P.A.
New Waterways	Inland Waterways Association	I.W.A. 1965
The Regent's Canal: A policy for its future	Regent's Canal Group	R.C.G. 1967
The Basingstoke Canal: The case for restoration	Surrey & Hampshire Canal Society and I.W.A.	I.W.A.
Canal & River Towpath Walks in the Home Counties	I.W.A.	I.W.A.
Guidebook to the River Wey	I.W.A.	I.W.A.
Introducing the Kennet & Avon Canal	Ray Denyer	K. & A. Canal Trust 1971
An Authentic Description of the Kennet & Avon Canal (reprint from 1811)	J. M. Richardson	K. & A. Canal Trust 1970
Stoke Bruerne Museum	British Waterways Board	B.W.B.

Boat clubs

An up to date list of all the clubs shown below, giving the current name and address of each honorary secretary, may be obtained from the British Waterways Board at Melbury House, Melbury Terrace. London NW1 6JX.

Bridgwater & Taunton Canal
Creech St. Michael Boating Club

Grand Union Canal (in geographical order of moorings from London to Birmingham)
St Pancras Cruising Club
Camden Boat Owners Association
West London Motor Cruising Club
Ealing Cruising Club
Uxbridge Cruising Club
Aylesbury Cruising Club
Islington Boat Club
Camden Boat Owners Association
West London Motor Cruising Club
Denham Cruising Club
Uxbridge Cruising Club
Aylesbury Pleasure Boat Club
Whitton Marina Cruising Club
Mid-Warwickshire Yacht Club
Black Buoy Cruising Club

Kennet & Avon Canal
Newbury Canoe Club
Pewsey Wharf Boat Club

Lee & Stort Rivers
Broxbourne Cruising Club
Lee & Stort Cruising Club
Rammey Marsh Cruising Club

Monmouthshire & Brecon Canal
Govilon Boat Club
Goytre Boat Owners Assn.

Oxford Canal
Coventry Cruising Club

Severn Navigation
Gloucester Yacht Club
Gloucester Rowing Club
Ketch Cruising Club
Lenchford Sailing Club
Worcester Rowing Club
Sabrina Cruising Club
Severn Motor Yacht Club

Societies

The Inland Waterways Association Ltd is 'the' national society of canal enthusiasts. It is the oldest, biggest and most energetic canal society and has permanent offices and staff. It has 7000 members and publishes a regular Waterways 'Bulletin'. Its address for details of membership is 114 Regents Park rd, London NW1 8UQ.

Other, mostly local, canal societies in the South – most of which are affiliated to the IWA – include those listed below.

East Anglian Waterways Association
Exeter Maritime Museum
Grand Union Canal Society
Kennet and Avon Canal Trust
Newport (Mon.) Canal Preservation Society
Old Union Canals Society
Railway and Canal Historical Society
Regent's Canal Group
Risca Magor & St. Mellons Canal Preservation Society
Somerset Inland Waterways Society
Southampton Canal Society
Stroudwater Canal Society
Surrey and Hampshire Canal Society

An up to date list, giving the current name and address of each honorary secretary, of all the societies shown above may be obtained from the British Waterways Board publication 'Waterway Users' Companion'. BWB, Melbury House, Melbury terrace, London NW1 6JX.

BWB Offices

Headquarters

Melbury House, Melbury Terrace, London NW1 6JX (01-262 6711) General and official enquiries and correspondence.

Willow Grange, Church road, Watford, Herts. (Watford 26422) Pleasure craft licences and registration, mooring permits and angling enquiries.

London Area Engineer

7th Floor, Gresham House, 53 Clarendon road, Watford, Herts. (31363). Responsible for the following maintenance yards.

Apsley Apsley lock, Ebberns road, Hemel Hempstead, Herts. (56910)

Enfield Ordnance road, Enfield lock, Middlesex. (Waltham Cross 64626).

Gayton Gayton Junction, near Blisworth, Northants. (Northampton 858233).

Limehouse Basin The pierhead offices, Narrow street, London E14 (01-790 3444). Advice on tides and opening times of the shiplock from the Regent's Canal and Lee and Stort navigation into the Thames at Limehouse.

Norwood Norwood Top Lock, Poplar avenue, Southall, Middlesex. (01-574 1220).

Thrupp Thrupp, Kidlington, Oxford. (Kidlington 2222).

Tring Bulbourne Workshops, Bulbourne, near Tring. Herts. (Tring 5938).

Birmingham Area Engineer

Reservoir House, Icknield Port road, Birmingham B16 0AA (021-454 7091). Responsible for the following maintenance yards.

Hatton Canal lane, Hatton, Warwick.

Hillmorton Hillmorton locks, Rugby, Warwicks. (Rugby 2393).

Gloucester Area Engineer

Dock Office, Gloucester (25524). Responsible for maintaining the waterways listed below, via the BWB Section Inspector or Foreman at the maintenance yards on those canals.

Swansea Canal 47 Hebson road, Clydach, Swansea. (3522).

Severn Navigation Diglis Lock, Worcester (356264).
Gloucester & Sharpness Canal Dock Office, Sharpness (348).
Brecon & Abergavenny Canal Canal Office, Govilon (Gilwern 830328).
Bridgwater & Taunton 23 George street, Rowbarton, Taunton (North Curry 363

Kennet & Avon Canal Canal Lock, Devizes (2859).
Lower Wharf, Padworth, Reading (Woolhampton 2277).

Miscellaneous

Bulls Bridge Repair Yard Bulls Bridge, Hayes road, Southall, Middlesex (01-573 2368).

Uxbridge Yard 23A Waterloo road, Uxbridge, Middlesex. (01-573 8231). (Evenings Uxbridge 32721). Dry dock available for hire.

Paddington The Canal Office, Delamere terrace, Paddington, London W2. (01-286 6101). For enquiries on the London canals, moorings, Zoo Waterbus trips and private party hire.

Stoke Bruerne The Waterways Museum (Roade 862229). Canal books, maps and souvenirs.

Canalphone 01-723 8487

A BWB service. 24 hr recorded message about stoppages and events on their southern waterways.

Index